D0433635

DESIGN PRINCIPLES

Six basic principles of design are now considered in turn as they apply to gardens. All are inextricably interrelated and they take up many of the topics already discussed in this chapter, offering a different angle on the design elements considered so far.

One way and another these principles are fulfilled in most successful gardens, from grand country estates to tiny urban oases. They are the rules that have guided the creation of the ideal designs in the next chapter. It is not always easy to start a design with something as abstract as a principle, but they are concepts to bear in mind, and are most useful as informal tests to apply to your design sketches and ideas – a sort of checklist of desirable criteria to measure how good a design idea is going to be.

The style and atmosphere of this garden combine country-house and cottage-garden themes. Although it contains a number of different features as well as a wealth of exuberant planting, a coherent design produces a balanced, well-structured picture.

A series of rope-swagged wooden pillars define the left-hand boundary of the vista, and climbing roses and a lavender hedge decorate this framework in suitably romantic style. The 'riot' of roses and perennials that spills out of the main border is kept in proportion by contrastingly simple features, such as the green arch of vines and the grassy path terminating in a statue, a focal point in harmony with the lyrical spirit of the garden.

SIMPLICITY

Simplicity brings with it a sense of calm. This quality is necessary for the restorative, peaceful atmosphere desirable in a garden intended for relaxation.

Making a simple garden design – or rather keeping a design simple – is not easy. It is largely a matter of organization, both of ideas and of the elements in the garden itself. You need to be decisive about the overall scheme you create: a garden has the quality of simplicity when a strong design has one clearly stated theme that conveys its message at first glance. This is not to say that all should be revealed immediately – there can be more to the garden than is seen when first looking (see 'interest' below). Simplicity need not lack depth and complexity, but these elements should be organized in a coherent fashion.

An overall disciplined approach will plan 'calm' areas to offset more eventful ones. For instance, if planting is full of colour and interest, keep adjacent surfaces low-key, with building materials in muted tones and paving in simple uncluttered patterns.

Simplicity is especially important in a small garden, where too many elements will make the scene fussy and contrived. Moreover, clutter makes a space seem smaller. Indecisive people are tempted to have 'a little of everything', and the result is a mess. However, simplicity is also important in larger plots, where the eye needs help and direction to find its way around. Don't confuse things by a jumble of contradictory lines and patterns. Keep each individual garden composition simple, but create a flow between the separate elements, linking the different areas in the picture into a whole.

A green pool of lawn provides a calm simple centre to a garden where layout and distinctive character make the most of a small rectangular plot. To one side, not seen here, a little 'woodland' path leads to a compact allee; in the foreground a small informal terrace opens off the house. Two tight balls of clipped box at the threshold of the terrace underpin the formal geometry of the lawn. Its shape is a smooth ellipse – incidentally, a figure that makes the space seem bigger by suggesting that you are seeing a circular lawn in perspective. Flower colour around the lawn is restricted to blues and pinks; planting on the terrace has a similar simple and economical theme.

UNITY AND HARMONY

These qualities are somewhat easier to find in a successful existing garden than to plan for at the outset. Quite often unity and harmony are absent in the early stages of creating a garden, when plants have not grown up enough to fill intended spaces and soften severe lines and raw new surfaces. The 'hard' elements of the landscape make an instant effect, but plants take longer. Finding these qualities in your new layout calls for patience. One way of envisaging them in a projected design is to imagine what you would like the garden to look and feel like in a few years' time, and then to 'translate' this atmosphere back into your plans.

To evoke an image of harmony, think of a mature, established garden in which there is an attractive continuity between the materials and style of the house. The plant colours and forms complement both one another and the adjacent structural elements. Where there is some new element, some surprise, such as a patch of seasonal bedding or a brightly planted container, this seems entirely in context. Where there is a transition to some special-purpose area in another part of the garden, it seems to occur naturally. By means of the routing of paths, the direction of paving joint lines, the positioning of archways and such intrinsic elements of the design, the layout directs you on a natural, rather than signposted tour around the garden.

Another harmonious image might be one of a garden following a Japanese theme with an arrangement of water, rocks, gravel with bamboos, azaleas, acers and other suitable planting. Picture this set against the backdrop of a clean-lined modern building whose materials offer no clash of cultures. There may be wooden decking, or simple paving. The elements are all simple and in keeping with each other.

There are several lessons to be drawn from these examples. In each, the hard elements of the garden relate harmoniously with the building and have a continuity, either of style or materials; often they will also tie in with the surrounding landscape – for example, when a local kind of stone is used for walls or paving. The timber elements work well together in terms of style and finish – whether naturally rustic or neatly manicured and perhaps painted. Don't opt for a particular type of paving simply because you like it – ask if it is appropriate. Does its hard geometric line fit with the soft rounded forms used elsewhere in the garden, for example?

When considering the planted elements of the garden, harmonious colour themes are perhaps the most obvious aspect to plan for. As you look at real gardens and photographs of others in books and magazines, make notes of effects that please you, and see if the plants used will flourish in your site. When indigenous trees in the landscape beyond the garden are well in view, it is a good idea to plant native species on the perimeter to ease the transition between the exotics within the garden and the 'natural' world outside.

When a garden is literally a unit – for example if it is too small to compartmentalize, or you don't wish to do so – something like a simple geometrical layout reinforces that very unity, and fulfils the criterion of simplicity. In a larger layout, the same shapes used in different areas and repeated plants can hold the different elements together, creating a rhythm or a theme. Independent elements in the garden thus contribute harmoniously to the whole: unity is an imaginary thread, tying them all together.

Left *Beautiful objects are an embodiment of the qualities of unity and harmony. This handsome urn nestling among foliage provides a perfect focal point in a quiet corner of the garden, where visitors can pause and study its effect. Its timeless shape is a fitting object of contemplation, of the sort deliberately included in classically inspired gardens. There are particularly pleasing harmonies between the urn and its surroundings. The pinkish tone of the clay is picked up in the nearby flower heads, and the muted sheen of the glaze is echoed in the leathery textures of the leaves.*

Above *This view of a summerhouse demonstrates how elusive the principle of united harmony can be. All the ingredients in the picture – plants, structures and materials – are different from one another. The design is asymmetrical, and there is no repeating motif or theme. Yet the beautifully balanced, spacious arrangement and, in particular, the restrained use of colour in the planting and the man-made elements, where pale shades of green, grey and beige predominate, create a calm, unified picture.*

BALANCE

Taken in its extreme form of symmetry, balance is best illustrated as, for example, a pair of identically planted urns flanking a flight of steps, or four clipped evergreens punctuating the corners of a square pool. Asymmetrical balance is less easy to define, more intuitive. It is what you find in flower arranging or painting when the artist organizes the elements according to the hidden law corresponding to the balancing of a pair of scales, where a larger, lighter mass of material is equivalent in value to the smaller, denser block of a weight. Discussion of aesthetic 'balance' draws on this terminology and often uses words like mass and weight metaphorically.

In the garden context, balance might mean avoiding placing a heavy emphatic element at one side or one end of a garden picture without compensating for it in some way at the other. It is not necessarily a question of matching it with something identical: a building like a gazebo might balance a small group of trees because it has a similar 'mass' or an equivalent visual 'value'.

Balance is more difficult to achieve in some places than others. Gardens that slope across the main view can seem to fall away or collapse down the hill into the next property. In this instance, balance can often be achieved by placing taller features or plants on the lower side. Structure or plants on higher ground will always tend to dominate those lower down, so planning should aim to counteract this.

Balance in planting takes into account factors such as size, overall shape or profile, and texture. Thus a solid-seeming evergreen is 'heavier' than a frothy, light-textured deciduous tree even if they are of the same size, and a balanced picture might match a single or smaller example of the first category with several, perhaps larger, specimens of the latter. There is colour balance to consider, too, particularly among flowering plants, but since flower colour is often short-lived, the leaf colour, shape and overall effect of the plant becomes part of the balance of the equation.

There is a designer's rule of thumb that advocates grouping plants and trees in odd numbers – threes, fives and so on. Curiously, this often works well, but the formula need not be adhered to slavishly. Balanced spacing between the elements is more important. It is easy in formal arrangements where equal distances can be measured, but calculating them by eye in an informal grouping is a more artistic process. The challenge is increased by the fact that you have to make allowances for the time factor and picture your saplings as full-grown trees. A two-dimensional plan will not help much in predicting these effects, so thumbnail sketches, no matter how crude – perhaps using photographs of the site as a background – will be useful to determine how to achieve balance with these vertical elements.

Above An elegant wooden seat is the centrepoint of a perfectly balanced picture. On either side, two large matching pots add weight to the design, with white flowers bringing light to a shady area and two fastigiate evergreens acting as sentinels. Two areas of basket-weave brickwork edge a herring-bone path whose rich pattern echoes the pattern on the seat back.

Right A curving path and terrace paved in brick make a platform which acts as a counterweight to the solid mass of the house and separates it from the moat-like pool. Two circular panels balance asymmetrically, their concentric rings of bricks providing the logic and the scale for the curving pattern of the path as it rounds the corner of the house.

SCALE AND PROPORTION

Getting this principle right is a matter of ensuring that the various elements (planting and man-made structures, horizontal and vertical) are all the appropriate size – for each other, and for the garden overall.

It is easier to demonstrate poor proportions than to point out good ones. Oversized elements will stand out as excessive; elements in proportion will simply look right. A large weeping willow, an overgrown conifer, a hedge of Leyland cypress allowed to soar unchecked – all of these will dwarf a small house and its garden. A paving area too large for the size of the plot will leave little space for grass and plants, and the mean borders that surround it will emphasize this lack. Without enough space for imaginative touches, the atmosphere of such a garden will appear efficient but dull.

At the other end of the scale, elements may be too small to be in proportion, creating a trivial, bitty effect. A small half-moon or circular bed will appear lost and meaningless in a very large expanse of grass and will not bear any relationship to the overall scheme. Narrow borders around a garden may be too small to grow plants of any stature, so leaving boundaries largely uncovered, and perhaps aggravating a sense of enclosure. Uncomfortably narrow paths that necessitate walking single file rather than permitting easy strolling side by side will seem completely out of proportion in a garden where there is plenty of space for wider ones.

An example of good proportion might be a broad terrace or patio that seems generous and gives the house the visual 'base' it needs while not taking up too much garden space. A formal panel of lawn or paving in a rectangle of garden will be a reasonable size if it echoes the shape overall without either overfilling it or making an insignificant gesture and looking like a label stuck somewhere in the middle. In an informal layout, a generously contoured expanse of grass curving between shrubs or beds strikes a happy balance between a wall-to-wall carpeting of lawn and a mere grass path between beds that are uncomfortably close.

Scale and proportion permeates every inch of a garden. Paving units, for example, should be in proportion with the area: small units in a large area may look fussy (bricks are perhaps the exception); very large paving slabs in a tiny space may make it look smaller. Similar considerations apply to vertical constructions, such as the posts and rafters of a pergola or archway; these have to be in proportion with its overall bulk to make a graceful design.

You can work out the practicalities of scale and proportion of the horizontal, flat elements of a layout fairly reliably in plan form on paper. You can sketch man-made verticals, such as fences and pergolas, accurately, too. More difficulty arises with plants, especially the larger trees and shrubs. When planning what to plant from scratch, take into account the ultimate spread as well as the height. Choose an appropriate variety carefully, and don't accept a substitute with a markedly different habit as second choice. Of course, it is vital to select from good nursery catalogues whose plant identification is reliable. You can sometimes make amends by tailoring an oversized tree or shrub to size, but some trees and conifers will not respond to heavy pruning later; even if they survive major trimming, you can ruin their shapes.

Of course if you are careful, you can plan compositions that break these 'rules' and still work, and, for example small gardens certainly don't need everything scaled down with miniature roses, alpine versions of herbaceous plants and so on. Occasionally a large-scale plant is the making of a small plot – something with a bold shape and large sculptural leaves. Equally there is a place for smaller items in large gardens: either placed within individual compartments, or generously grouped and massed so that they are in proportion.

This perfectly proportioned planting scheme, with the tall spires of Ligularia przewalskii *balanced by the dramatic round forms of* Darmera peltata, *provides an attractive frame for a path winding through the garden. The scale and arrangement of the borders and the architectural elements – in particular, the wooden pergola planted with wisteria – combine to make a shaded passageway that invites exploration. The planting surrounding the path is predominately of bold foliage, with a few bright colours – of ligularia, pelargoniums and fuchsias – providing the necessary accents, and the jewel-like flashes of pink impatiens and blue lobelia brightening the passageway and beckoning the visitor on.*

INTEREST

A garden may combine all the previous principles of design and not be quite successful enough because it is simply dull: it lacks interest.

What is defined as interesting is to some extent in the eye of the beholder. Even in the most functional vegetable plot, the keen visitor might find some succulent item to focus on, while the casual observer can marvel at the pattern of the neat rows and the forms of the plants. Some people are fascinated by categories of plants that others find boring. In a garden designed for pleasure the whole purpose is to provide interest and enjoyment. As we have seen, focal points are important in making well-designed garden compositions. Water features might be the perfect focus for some gardeners; others will have statues, sculpture or ornaments.

A dictionary definition of interest is 'to arouse or hold the attention or curiosity'. One thing that arouses curiosity is some sense of mystery, creating a desire to explore and find out what is around the corner or behind the screen, and where a twisting path or hidden archway leads. What attracts and then holds the attention is a focal point. The interaction of these two elements creates movement around a garden and provides the explorer with a series of rewards. Without a focal point or an element of intrigue, a garden will not be interesting, no matter how well-balanced it is.

A garden that can be seen in its entirety at one glance leaves no surprises to discover, no mystery to unravel. In all but the smallest gardens, mystery can be implied, by a trellis screen or carefully placed feature or plant that obscures some potentially secret corner, tempting the human appetite for that which is intriguing and drawing people into the garden to enjoy the different viewpoints that moving around any space will naturally provide.

Plant interest is high in this small garden with its rich tapestry of shrubs, climbers and favourite cottage-garden perennials. The scale of the planting makes no concession to the plot's extreme narrowness: it is generous and expansive, drawing plant lovers to investigate its treasures. The partly hidden seat and the darker depths beyond the urn on the lawn provide additional lures and invitations to explore.

PERFORMANCE

Another name for this rather unorthodox-sounding principle might be 'fulfilment of requirements'. Though last on the list, it is important. As has been said at the beginning, a garden that does not meet its owners' and users' needs must be deemed poorly designed. The adage 'form must follow function' is certainly true of gardens. A business couple will not be pleased with a labour-intensive garden, however beautiful, if their requirement was somewhere to relax in their spare time. A plant enthusiast, on the other hand, will not be satisfied with a plot covered entirely with paving or grass.

When you are planning your own garden, the test of the design is whether it contains the elements and fits the purposes that you set down on the check list as discussed at the beginning of this chapter. Of course, your original ideas may well have been modified by the constraints of what is possible within the given site and your budget, but within these limits the design should fulfil the requirements you want from your garden.

This decorative little garden functions as an efficient outdoor living space, perfect for relaxing and entertaining and as charmingly furnished as the rooms inside the house. Paving underfoot frees the owners to devote time to the flowering plants they prefer instead of tending a fiddly patch of lawn. Elegant white furniture is practical and sustains the theme of the predominantly white flowers – whose scent makes the atmosphere of the garden especially enjoyable in the evenings.

GARDEN PLANS

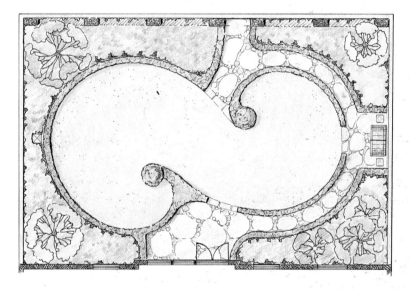

This chapter puts the elements and principles of garden design in context, showing what good designs look like on paper and how to visualize them in three dimensions.

These plans give design solutions for the most common shapes and sizes of plot, offering several approaches for each and exploring them in depth. A perspective drawing in colour brings the garden alive in three-dimensional detail alongside a coloured plan that clarifies the layout. Explanatory text gives a clear account of the design reasons behind the key elements. Following each of the main designs are black-and-white plans showing alternative layouts that are, for example, easier to maintain or in a different style or that fit a site with slightly different dimensions.

SMALL SQUARE GARDENS

There are many exquisite little square gardens that succeed, in spite of the restrictions imposed by limited space, because thoughtful planning has produced a coherent and harmonious picture. Good organization lies behind making the most of a small area. It is not only a matter of choosing a clear design theme and implementing that: equally important is eliminating distractions and clutter. With space at a premium, every single plant or constructional element must earn its place in the scheme of things.

As the following pages show, designs for small square gardens span a range of styles from crisp formality, where 'hard' landscaping predominates, to plant-filled informality. As a rule in small gardens, it is best to opt for a style that is either formal or informal rather than something in between, which is liable simply to result in a muddle.

Garden styles

Generally speaking, a formally based design is most likely to succeed in making a small square plot seem spacious. It enables you to use man-made surfaces for space-enhancing effects, such as laying paving diagonally or in circular patterns to counteract the box-like feeling of the square. Formal layouts, too, can often incorporate surrounding walls and fences into the garden architecture, making the physical boundary an integral part of the planned effect.

With designs aimed to appear 'natural', on the other hand, space is lost disguising or hiding the boundaries. For an informal style to be completely successful, careful planting of trees, shrubs and climbers has to mask the regular shape entirely, since it is difficult to accept a garden that is supposed to be natural against an obvious backdrop of fencing or brickwork. The informal design on pages 46–7 uses wattle hurdles to disguise the parts of the boundary visible between plants. This informal layout also shows how a strong, positive overall approach makes a virtue of the lack of space, turning a tour of the garden into an exploration of hidden regions.

Most small square plots, however, are designed to make a single garden 'room'. Firstly, sheer shortage of space on the ground leaves little scope for compartmentalizing, although the family garden on page 44 suggests an intriguing way of designating separate areas for different uses. Secondly, the boundaries may enclose the garden space in a way that gives the sensation of walls enclosing a room. The surrounding wall or fence may itself be high, or you might add extra height in the guise of planting or trellis to ensure privacy. Inevitably, the higher the surround, the smaller the area within it appears and the greater the amount of shade cast – nearby buildings or trees may increase that problem.

Fortunately, some excellent and handsome plants will thrive in shade (see pages 155–7 for some suggestions). Tall boundaries contribute additional vertical planting space for glorious effects with climbers. They can also be enhanced with architectural features such as archways, perhaps deliberately creating a *trompe-l'oeil* illusion. Both the pergola in the plantsman's garden on page 44 and the herb garden's mirror-backed alcove on pages 48–9 add extra depth, implying that the garden extends further than it actually does. On a practical level, you can maximize space by planning features to play a dual role. A low retaining wall may be wide enough to use as a seat, for example. In the formal garden overleaf, seats have hinged lids and double as storage spaces, and planted containers conceal a barbecue.

Abundant planting hides the walls of this tiny courtyard, which is so full of interest that its small size is forgotten. Partly hidden by the jostling foliage, and so made more intriguing, are focal points such as the little statue. Leaves contrast richly in shape and texture, but flower colours are confined to reds and whites – a limited scheme suits such a small space.

THE FORMAL GARDEN

The plan for this small square garden takes up the theme of calm and restfulness. The style is asymmetrically formal, and provides plenty of space for relaxing and entertaining.

1 The central planter is the focus of the garden and is designed to be viewed from the house as well as from the timber seats. Its seasonal bedding grows in wedge-shaped fibre-glass containers; these can be lifted out to reveal a barbecue beneath.

2 The paving is pale blue-grey, a colour that reflects light and thereby gives a sense of space. Blue setts are used for all the edgings and play an important role in linking the various elements of the garden together.

3 The timber seats are positioned in sun and have hinged tops, thereby doubling as storage cupboards. The raised borders surrounding the seating area reduce, visually, the height of the outer walls, and the bricks of their retaining walls match those of the boundary, thus providing a feeling of continuity.

4 The lawn has been planted with a shade-tolerant grass seed mix. If this area is very small, a low evergreen ground cover, such as a small-leaved ivy or *Arenaria balearica*, would be a suitable alternative and would provide a more textured surface.

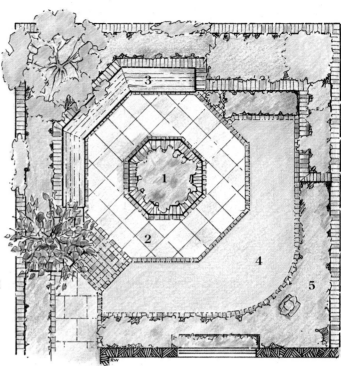

5 The shady corner where the boundary and house walls meet contrasts with the lighter atmosphere of the rest of the garden. It is enlivened by a piece of sculpture which is positioned to be seen from the paved area across the light expanse of lawn.

A pool with a small fountain could be the central feature of the garden, in place of the raised bed covering the barbecue. This would give the area a more spacious feel – though it would, of course, be unsuitable in a garden where very young children play.

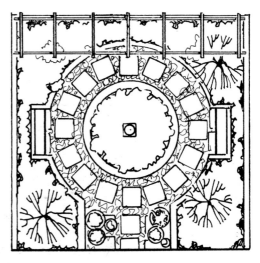

A low-maintenance garden
The main focal point of this symmetrical easy-care garden is a raised pool and wall-mounted fountain. Planting is confined to raised beds and square pots or planters. A curved seat, set partially into and against the right-hand retaining wall, looks towards a secondary focal point, perhaps a vase or sculpture. The ground is entirely paved and would therefore need only to be swept to keep the garden looking well-kept. Plenty of space is available for entertaining and children's play.

A plantsman's garden
This neat and symmetrical garden is given over almost entirely to beds and borders; even the paving stones are surrounded by a carpeting of low-level plants. The central circular bed and those at the periphery can either be raised for ease of maintenance or set level with the surrounding paving. Two seats positioned opposite each other face the central focal point.

The pergola at the far end of the garden is covered with rambling plants and lends a sense of depth to the space.

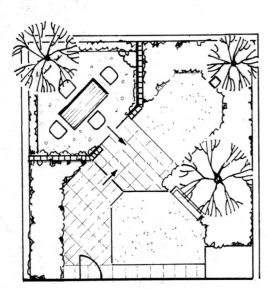

A family garden
This assymetrical design is divided into small connecting 'rooms', to suit a variety of family needs. The house door leads directly on to paving that changes direction as it reaches a step.

To the left, the paving leads to an enclosed area for relaxation; its seclusion is created by a timber screen covered with climbing plants. The table and chairs are permanently in position. To the right is an area of grass with a focal point at its far end beneath a small tree.

Looking back towards the house, a bench seat is tucked into a corner of another grassy area. Tools and other equipment are stored in a garden cupboard at the near right-hand corner, reached by a narrow path.

A raised pool in baroque style makes a strong focal point, as in the plan for the low-maintenance garden (opposite). Its bold curves in both horizontal and vertical planes contrast splendidly with the regularity of a square plot. The classical combination of water, cool stonework and foliage plants creates a mood of calm; its well-ordered appearance calls for relatively little effort. Clipped shrubs in pots – another keynote of the formal garden – can be grouped in different positions to ring the changes.

THE INFORMAL GARDEN

This tiny town garden has been planned as a natural oasis in the middle of the city, deliberately enclosed and with a jungle atmosphere. The boundaries are disguised by wattle hurdles and tall bold plants. Although it is so small, parts of the garden are hidden from each other, and exploring it seems like an adventure. Comparatively heavy planting for year-round interest fills the beds and helps create the distinct areas.

Harmonious sculptural forms can be achieved using natural materials, such as boulders set in gravel or pebbles. This kind of arrangement works best when the boulder and gravel are of the same stone type, giving an effect of natural erosion.

1 Setts of natural stone are used as paving – and edging – throughout the garden. They provide a strong sense of continuity, linking the garden's separate areas without detracting from its informality. Grass or other ground cover grows within the joints of the paving,

softening the appearance while still allowing a reasonably dry and safe walking surface for most of the year.

2 The circular seating area is positioned in the sunniest part of the garden, although it is partly shaded by the surrounding planting which ensures its seclusion. A carefully placed small tree prevents the area being overlooked from the neighbouring garden. A flowering tree, such as *Catalpa bignonioides* or its yellow form 'Aurea', screens the area from the house and contributes both to the structure and to the attractiveness of the garden.

3 A circular pool, partially sunken, brings reflected light to a dark corner, forming an interesting focal point from the seating area while remaining an intriguing secret from the house. A weeping tree placed in the corner adds to the air of tranquillity; one that has flowers as well, such as *Prunus* 'Pendula', is a good choice.

4 A small clearing, laid with gravel or pebbles makes another partly hidden area. It contains a sculptural arrangement of rounded rocks and boulders; the plants growing behind act as a foil, while only a few grow within the arrangement so as not to spoil its simplicity. The gravel or pebbles are contained by an edging of setts which is partially obscured by the surrounding planting, thus keeping the air of informality.

A family garden
In this version, a more open area has been created, making it suitable for a lawn – tiny patches of grass can be a nuisance – and children's play. The feel of the garden is more spacious, although parts remain deliberately screened from view.

At the far end a gazebo or open summerhouse forms the principal seating area. From here the main view is directed diagonally across the lawn to a focal point – perhaps a sculptural piece or a distinctive plant. Curved beds and trees hide all this from the house: all that can be seen is a small space of terrace and lawn, a conifer planted as a lawn specimen, and the surrounding planting. A path made of the same flat natural stone as the terrace curves under the conifer and leads invitingly to the hidden area beyond.

THE HERB GARDEN

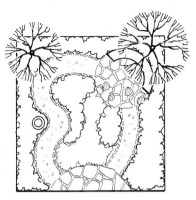

Historically, herb gardens are associated with formal layouts, which this symmetrical design fittingly reflects. A small enclosed garden is a perfect environment for growing herbs and other aromatic plants which are often native to countries with warm climates. Here, sheltering walls and well-drained raised beds provide ideal growing conditions. The brick paving makes a warm, static ground cover that, together with the brick walls, unifies the whole design.

1 The terrace nearest the house is laid in a herring-bone pattern, which has a softer effect than the straighter lines in the central section of the garden. In the raised beds on either side, an apple and a pear tree add height and continue the culinary theme. Two Versailles or similar square planters, whose colour echoes the distant pavilion, are filled with rosemary – one of the more modern upright forms would be best in this setting.

2 The central raised bed with low-growing herbs contains a sundial, which is positioned low down so as not to draw too much attention away from the pavilion beyond. It is, nevertheless, the garden's

A carefully placed mirror can give a welcome illusion of greater depth and space in a small garden. It is important to soften the edges with surrounding foliage and flowers that overlap the mirror and create the impression of the planting continuing into the distance.

centrepiece, and is meant to be appreciated during a leisurely walk around it. Four clipped bay trees form 'sentinels' that punctuate the main corners formed by the surrounding retaining walls. They are grown in terracotta pots that harmonize with the brick work.

3 A mirrored arch, set in a recess, makes an interesting *trompe l'oeil*; it reflects light and creates a feeling of space on a shady wall. On the opposite wall, for balance, is a circular window shape. This could either be an opening in the wall, if practicable, or another recessed mirror to reflect the arch opposite.

4 The pavilion and seat beneath form the main focal point of the garden, particularly when viewed from the house, and provide a romantic and restful place to sit. Climbing plants trail over the top of the pavilion from the trellis-work on either side and add depth and the chance for a profusion of colour at greater height.

An informal alternative
Here the house door leads on to an area of natural, randomly laid stone paving. A brick- or timber-edged path of gravel, which associates well with the herbs, leads to the seating area and then back again round to the house. The seating area is circular and again made of random stone paving, with a semi-circular stone seat set upon it. Carpeting plants such as creeping thyme are allowed to grow in the gaps between the stones, providing fragrance and a softness underfoot.

Other low-growing plants fill the central space, permitting a view in either direction. Larger plants grow around the periphery of the garden, offering greater privacy. Fruit trees, too, conceal what might otherwise be visually intrusive corners, while providing welcome shade.

The garden's focal point is formed by a piece of sculpture or a terracotta jar. The path curves naturally and yet dramatically around it, so giving added interest to the walkway.

SMALL RECTANGULAR GARDENS

Small rectangular gardens are probably more numerous than any other type, especially in towns and suburbs, and a small rectangle is one of the simplest and most versatile shapes to design. You can partition it easily into two separate areas to suit different purposes, like the family garden on pages 52–3 or the cottage garden on pages 62–63; this also creates, visually, the impression of more space – by keeping a part hidden, you are invited to explore. On the other hand, this kind of garden is sufficiently compact and well-proportioned to be simply treated as a whole, as in the plan on page 55 or those on pages 56–7, with an open central area (given privacy, perhaps, by screening trees), and a unified design or planting theme.

A unified style

A degree of unity is always important in the design of small gardens, and it is a mistake to try to squeeze too much in. A good idea is to link separate areas with some overall theme, such as by using the same path materials. Particularly if the boundaries are handsome walls or fences, you can employ a restrained and formal style, making full use of the good proportions of the rectangle. The garden on pages 56–7 bases a formal layout on a dignified theme using an ellipse. A more casual and informal approach is equally possible. The family garden on pages 52–3 has an asymmetrical design in which formal structures are softened by luxuriant planting. It is more difficult to go for a completely natural-looking informality with this shape; as with small square plots, disguising the existence of formal boundaries altogether can be difficult.

Sloping gardens

Rectangular gardens are often set on a sloping site; this presents exciting design challenges, shown on pages 58–61. One of the most satisfying solutions is to create the garden on two levels. Nearest the house, you can design a flat area which acts as a useful extension of the indoor space. Depending which way (and how steeply) the ground slopes, this can make an intimate enclosed area with a bank rising beyond, or a terrace on which the house sits, with the ground falling away below it.

If the change of level removes part of the garden from sight, it is possible to plan for a decisively different atmosphere in each part, and the embankment or retaining wall itself becomes something that you will want to treat creatively. In a garden set into a steep slope the carving out of flat ground next to the house makes a potential courtyard area, complete with facing 'wall' that you can drape with climbers and set with hanging containers and statuary. You can use steps up to the higher level to issue an invitation to explore and make interesting diagonal lines in the composition.

When the garden slopes downwards from the house, even above quite a shallow drop, the ground below may be out of sight when you are sitting down. You may want to have some kind of parapet wall or rail, especially if you are thinking of children's safety, although the higher and more solid the safety barrier the more it will contribute a feeling of containment. Depending on whether the outlook offers a ravishing view of blue distance or a more intrusive landscape of other people's homes, you can make the design elements frame the view or draw the eye down towards absorbing features in the garden below.

Simplicity is the principle behind the design of this small rectangular garden, though it offers plenty of interest. The massed shrubs and herbaceous plants in the border are balanced by an uncluttered expanse of lawn. With foliage creeping forwards to soften the lines of the stone-flagged path and steps, these ingredients suggest the leisured atmosphere of a country-house garden in miniature. The curving path and partly hidden seating area offer an irresistible invitation to explore. Screening trees disguise the far boundary of the garden.

THE FAMILY GARDEN

This earthenware bird bath is framed by the rose arch to make an attractive low-level focal point.

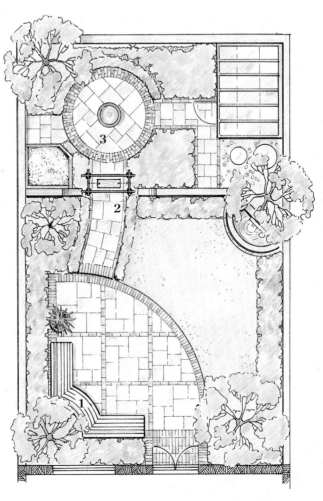

In order to accommodate a family's different needs, this garden is divided in two. Carefully placed walls shield the more functional area at the far end – which incorporates space for children's play and for vegetable growing – from the area nearest the house, designed for relaxation. The compartments are linked by the use of buff-brown paving stones and blue bricks in both areas.

1 The seating area, with its generous three-sided seat and wide terrace, establishes the predominant feeling of relaxation in this part of the garden.

The main axis here is diagonal, with a restful view across the lawn to a wall fountain and small pool, which form the garden's main focal point. The surrounding walls are white, making the garden seem always light and sunny; they are topped with coping stones that match the paving, adding to the sense of continuity throughout this garden.

2 The path from the seating area is gently curved to give a feeling of depth and space, leading the eye through a decorative wooden arch to a focal point beyond – here, an earthenware bird bath. The pretty rose-covered arch is sturdy enough to incorporate a swing (a hook on one side allows the swing to be hung out of the way when not in use).

3 The far end of the garden is designed for various activities and is almost completely hidden from the area for relaxation. The circular space where the paths meet can be used for children's play and there is a sandpit in the left-hand corner. For adults, there are beds for herbs and vegetable growing, and a lean-to glasshouse in the top right-hand corner.

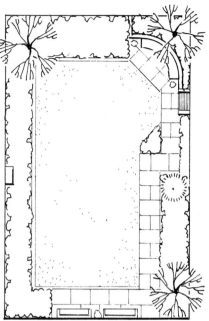

A low-maintenance garden

Whether it forms the functional opening in a dividing wall or hedge or is simply a free-standing hoop spanning a path, a plant-covered archway contributes an attractive vertical element to the garden composition. A path that leads through an arch gains a touch of mystery, and any plant groupings or focal points are enhanced by being glimpsed through a frame. Styles and materials can be chosen to suit the layout, from simple hoops or ornamental scrollwork in metal to more substantial wooden structures (as in the family garden shown on the previous pages).

A low-maintenance garden

Here the plot has been treated as one simple open area, leaving plenty of room for children's ball games. Most of the space is devoted to lawn, surrounded by paving or beds with recessed edges for easy mowing.

The seating area is at the far end of the garden and is backed by a raised bed with a curved edge enclosing the seat. From here the view is directed diagonally across the lawn to a tall focal point, which breaks up what might otherwise be a rather uniform expanse of wall.

Another interesting detail is provided by the path from the house, which changes direction round a flower bed and then continues towards a barbecue and the seating area.

A garden for young children

A garden designed for young children need not look like an adventure playground. Although this solution is not compartmentalized, carefully placed planting and the curving path create different areas, hiding some parts of the garden from the small seating area next to the house, and providing internal structure.

The path encircles a shrub-filled bed, making a 'round-about' and giving children a perfect tricycle track. It is made of random-shaped stone pieces that 'mould' to the curving shape more easily than would rectangular or square stones.

In the far corner is a good-sized area for play equipment, partly fenced off by a timber screen and surfaced with a soft paving material such as pine bark granules. There is room for a climbing frame, incorporating a swing, as well as a sandpit. Evergreen shrubs form the centre of the 'round-about' and help screen the play area. They provide structure and interest in the garden throughout the year.

A plantsman's garden

In this small rectangular garden the emphasis is on providing plenty of room for growing a range of favourite plants, both ornamental and vegetable, while leaving some space for relaxation and recreation. Here, the brick-paved seating area overlooks a lawn for children's play but is tucked away, surrounded by shrubs and trees to make it secluded.

From the house, the focal point is a small weeping tree, such as *Pyrus salicifolia* 'Pendula', grown as a lawn specimen. The brick path is seen to turn sharply out of sight, inviting further exploration. From the secluded patio, the eye is led along a gently curving path through an opening in the hedge to a focal point, such as a statue, set against an evergreen backdrop.

The clipped hedge, also evergreen, hides the functional vegetable plot, garden shed and small glasshouse.

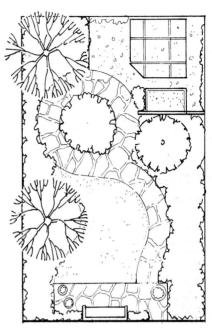

A garden for young children

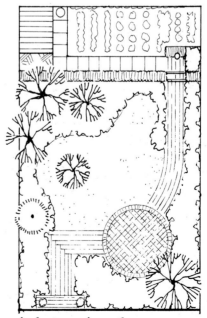

A plantsman's garden

THE FORMAL GARDEN

Formality need not imply hard lines, and an ellipse is a good shape to use in a rectangular plot. This design is based on a series of overlapping ellipses, which form the main ground pattern. The curving shapes bring a sense of calm but also of gentle movement round the garden. The design is strictly formal and symmetrical, with two strong intersecting axes running the length and breadth of the garden, giving four viewpoints from which the scene must be equally beautiful.

1 The curved terrace next to the house sets the tone of the whole garden and its attention to symmetry. An eyecatching bronze statue and a flower bed take up a significant amount of space and, though not seen from the house, this feature is necessary for the view from the far end of the garden. The terrace, and the paths, are made of small natural stone pieces set in mortar, with brick patterning and edges. The irregular stone shapes introduce a softer element.

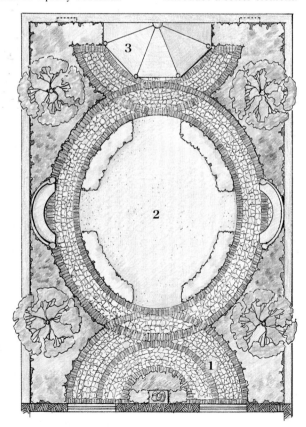

2 The central oval lawn is surrounded by low planting with four openings at the main axes – like windows for the four directional views. Semi-circular stone seats either side echo the curves of the design. At the four 'corners' of the central ellipse are matching cherry or apple trees.

3 The graceful pavilion sheltering a long, low seat has an oriental tone that matches the bronze statue. The open sides contribute a light and airy feeling (a similarly shaped aviary enclosed with netting would work as well). The wall behind continues the formal theme, with statues in niches either side of the pavilion. Indeed the surrounding walls as a whole are inherently formal and are mainly unadorned by climbing plants; rather they are used as foils for the shorter plants growing in front of them.

A terracotta figure set in each niche in the far wall emphasizes the formal, contemplative style of the garden.

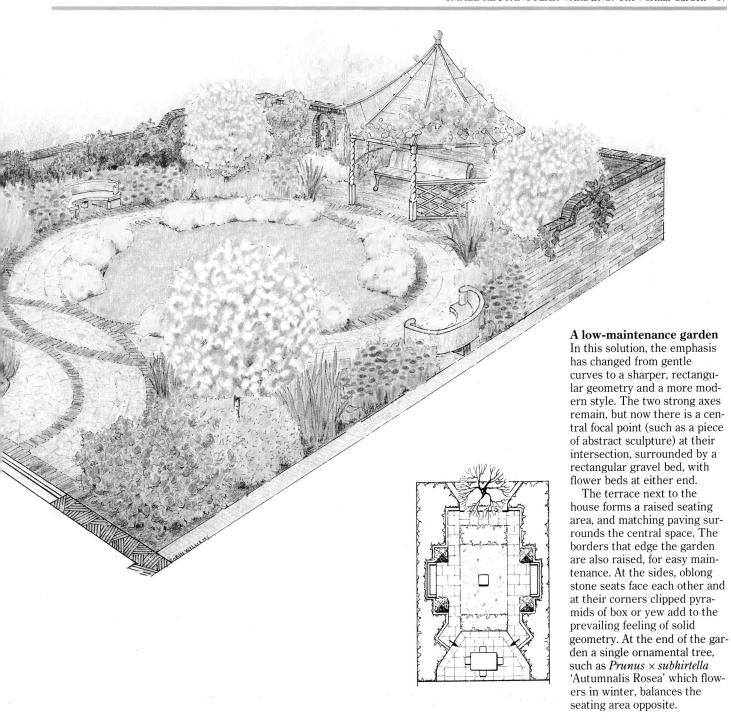

A low-maintenance garden

In this solution, the emphasis has changed from gentle curves to a sharper, rectangular geometry and a more modern style. The two strong axes remain, but now there is a central focal point (such as a piece of abstract sculpture) at their intersection, surrounded by a rectangular gravel bed, with flower beds at either end.

The terrace next to the house forms a raised seating area, and matching paving surrounds the central space. The borders that edge the garden are also raised, for easy maintenance. At the sides, oblong stone seats face each other and at their corners clipped pyramids of box or yew add to the prevailing feeling of solid geometry. At the end of the garden a single ornamental tree, such as *Prunus × subhirtella* 'Autumnalis Rosea' which flowers in winter, balances the seating area opposite.

THE SLOPING GARDEN

With this small site – as with many sloping gardens – much of it 'disappears' behind the embankment formed by excavating a level area next to the house. The aim is to overcome the problem of this small space appearing cramped: the terrace is designed to look light and spacious. Excursions to the upper level will be infrequent in winter, so a further aim is to make the area visible from the house as attractive as possible all year round. The advantage of having two levels is that they can be given completely different treatments without a clash of styles, since one cannot be seen from the other.

1 Pale-coloured paving
stones give a feeling of light
and space to the area next to
the house. They are laid in a
simple style – a more intricate
pattern would seem fussy and
make the area appear smaller.
Four pots planted for seasonal
colour are arranged symmetrically, and the matched seats
against the side walls contribute to the balanced effect.

**2 An ornamental pool and
fountain** whose water spouts
from a bronze shell set in an
oval niche, makes a handsome
centrepiece to the paved area.
This part of the garden has
been treated in a strictly formal way, with the features and
materials used providing the
year-round interest. The pool
surround is wide enough for
sitting and is made, like the
enclosed side walls and the
strong retaining wall behind it,
of an attractive combination of
brick and flint.

3 The central bed behind the
retaining back wall of the pool
contains low-growing plants
and shrubs so as not to make
the terrace too enclosed. Two
walkways curve either side:
steps to the left, and to the
right a more gently rising path
made of snapped flints with flat
facets uppermost. The path
enables heavy gardening
equipment to be taken to the
upper level, and the materials
provide some continuity with
the lower, while providing a
flatter, less 'cobbled' surface.

4 The upper level is designed
as a completely different garden, a soft retreat after the
somewhat austere formality of
the terrace. Indeed, since the
ground slopes, a formal style
would be inappropriate. The
flint path leads to a rustic
summerhouse overlooking an
'alpine' meadow. Surrounding
planting includes conifers and
heathers, in keeping with the
hilly ambience.

*The pool and fountain form the
main view from the house. A
feature like this would be
essential in any similar garden
to relieve an otherwise blank
retaining wall, and this works as
well in winter as summer.*

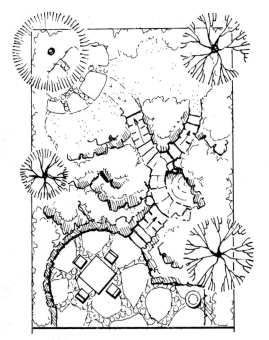

A rock garden

In this version, the sloping site has been treated as one, in an informal style. The whole garden gives the impression of a rocky hillside, as natural stone has been used everywhere: in the paving, in the steps up the garden and even in the retaining wall that curves round the seating area by the house. This wall has been made to look like a rockery, and stone slabs planted with alpines and shrubs continue the rockery up to a flatter meadow-like area. At the top is a second seating area sheltered by a tree.

The garden's main feature is a small pond in a rocky grotto, approached by steps up from the terrace. This grotto and the rockery look attractive from the house all year round.

A descending garden

In a smallish site that slopes downwards from the house, creating a flat area next to the house also brings problems – the bigger the terrace, the higher the retaining wall and the steeper the drop to the garden below. Here the paved area has been kept quite small, but the simple diagonal pattern of paving stones in one light material gives the impression of space, as does the circular area that juts out and is designed specifically for sitting to overlook the garden. A hand rail above the retaining wall allows a view of the garden from the house, although a parapet wall would be safer for children.

The steps to the lawn descend in a curve; these look more attractive and take up less space than would straight ones. On the right is a raised bed, its retaining wall curving with the steps and its height helping to screen the shed. Diagonally across from the stepping-stone path is a focal point, such as a statue, beneath a tree. A tall evergreen tree on one side, just below the retaining wall, and the raised bed on the other deliberately channel the view from the terrace into the plot below.

Above left *The transition between two levels of this sloping rock garden is simple and dramatic. An adventurous use of scale deploys just a few large boulders to suggest a rocky mountainside. A screen of jungly foliage separates the garden areas completely. Stone-edged steps paved with setts harmonize with the rocks while offering a reassuringly safe passage.*

Above *As with the descending garden (opposite), a circular terrace is approached by curving steps, though here, rather than winding round the seating area they lead up more directly beside a shallow embankment. This is covered with a fine combination of contrasting shapes of plant and leaf with a few touches of flower colour.*

The natural stone treads of the steps project slightly beyond the brick risers. This is both aesthetically pleasing and makes for safer going, as the edges stand out better in poor light.

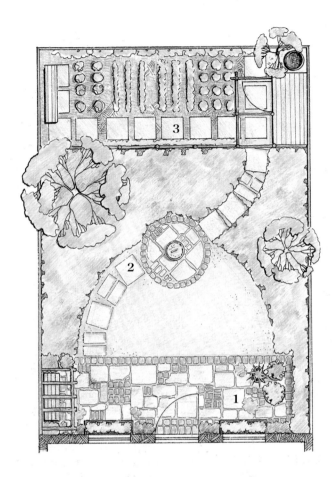

THE COTTAGE GARDEN

A rectangle is a convenient shape for a cottage garden, since a part can be cordoned off for the more utilitarian aspects of vegetable growing and storage, while leaving space for the more decorative plants. The problem with cottage gardens is that they can look messy – traditionally they are collections of annuals, perennials, herbs and roses, placed just anywhere and growing in happy confusion. Here, a firm design enables these plants to be placed within a structure that gives the garden some form, but makes it seem as if it has evolved naturally.

1 The paved area next to the house brings a feeling of maturity to the garden by the use of old setts, bricks and stone flags laid to make a tapestry effect. Moss or grass fills the joints, softening and easing the transition from paving to lawn. Adding to the deliberately old-fashioned, romantic atmosphere is an arbour made from rustic poles, covered with climbing roses and sheltering a seat. The picket fence – again deliberately chosen for its cottagey effect – that encloses the whole garden is taller around the paved area to give privacy.

2 The curved diagonal path of stepping stones is a strong structural element, linking both ends of the garden but in an informal way. At its centre is the main focal point, a sundial on a plinth, standing on a circle of tapestry-effect paving that links with the terrace. The semi-circular lawn, of either grass or camomile, is an essential setting for the 'happy confusion' of herbaceous plants. The beds contain a collection of cottage plants seemingly arranged at random – but with an eye to colour clashes. A fruit tree in the larger bed and an ornamental tree in the smaller add height – apple and lilac would be appropriate choices.

Rustic work makes attractive screens or windows to other parts of the garden, at the same time making excellent hosts to climbing plants, especially roses.

Suitable designs for the construction of panels are more or less endless, and this is an alternative to the one shown in the main illustration.

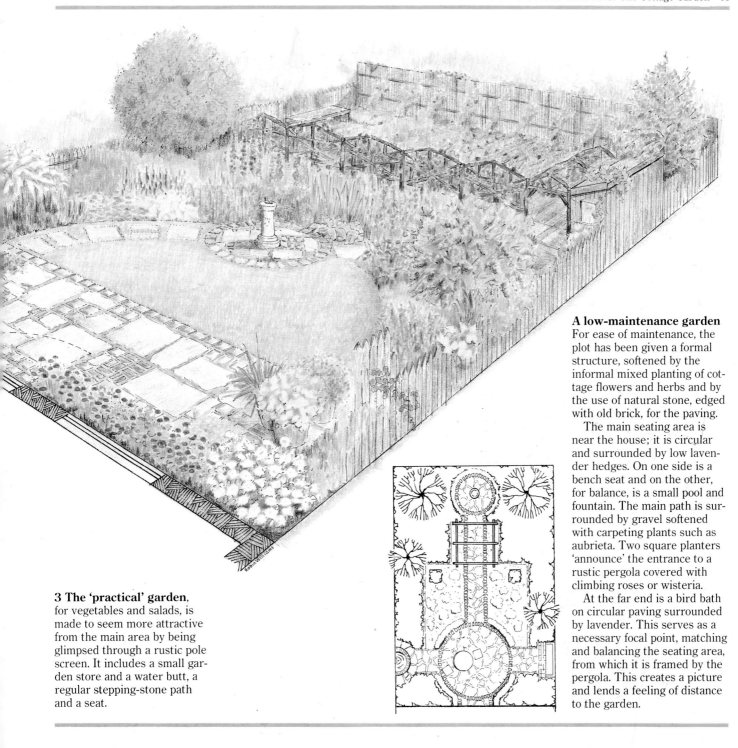

3 The 'practical' garden, for vegetables and salads, is made to seem more attractive from the main area by being glimpsed through a rustic pole screen. It includes a small garden store and a water butt, a regular stepping-stone path and a seat.

A low-maintenance garden
For ease of maintenance, the plot has been given a formal structure, softened by the informal mixed planting of cottage flowers and herbs and by the use of natural stone, edged with old brick, for the paving.

The main seating area is near the house; it is circular and surrounded by low lavender hedges. On one side is a bench seat and on the other, for balance, is a small pool and fountain. The main path is surrounded by gravel softened with carpeting plants such as aubrieta. Two square planters 'announce' the entrance to a rustic pergola covered with climbing roses or wisteria.

At the far end is a bird bath on circular paving surrounded by lavender. This serves as a necessary focal point, matching and balancing the seating area, from which it is framed by the pergola. This creates a picture and lends a feeling of distance to the garden.

LONG NARROW GARDENS

When a plot is extremely long in relation to its width, the garden is in danger of becoming no more than a corridor along which you seem to be hustled by an uncomfortably forceful sense of movement. One of the best, and in some ways the simplest, ways of avoiding this is to divide the plot into a succession of different garden areas. Each garden 'room' – more or less separate and more or less formally enclosed as you like – can have its own character and atmosphere.

Cleverly sited formal divisions give you control of the proportions of individual areas, allowing you to fill them with a symmetrical design based on a perfect square or circle, for instance. The compartmented garden on page 76 consists of three such regular rooms, while the family garden shown on pages 66–7 terminates in a single symmetrical compartment in the formal vegetable garden, reached through a series of more informal garden areas that flow naturally into one another. A design based on a series of curves (as in several of the gardens that follow) will both create interrelated garden areas and establish rounded shapes to contrast with the hard parallel lines of the boundaries.

If you divide a narrow garden into different areas you may be able to solve various problems with your site. It may be possible to position the 'barriers' to turn some existing feature such as an intrusively sited tree into an advantage, to screen and disguise something less than beautiful (a shed or telegraph pole in the garden, or a blot on the landscape beyond), or to coincide with a change of ground level, as in the gardens on pages 70–73.

Different styles and purposes

The succession of distinct areas provides you with physically separate spaces for accommodating a series of different items or activities – a vegetable plot, a greenhouse and shed, a children's play area, a water feature, an outdoor sitting or dining room. Or you can take advantage of the compartments to display different styles of planting – an informal or semi-wild corner here, a more strictly formal layout there. Compartments are used in some of the world's great gardens to contain distinctive colour themes that would otherwise clash or be diminished in impact, and this principle could provide you with inspiration on a smaller scale.

If you create divisions to counteract the directional pull of the corridor shape, you can also provide some overall sense of continuity, at least between successive areas. Keeping the material and style of the paths consistent makes a good link. It is a good idea to provide a 'reward' or reason for walking through the compartmented garden. You can make the last area worth visiting with a well-placed focal point, a seat, a *rond-point* (as in the vegetable garden on pages 66–7) or even a secret garden (as on pages 74–5).

Of course, there are alternatives to making separate enclosures in order to disguise the narrowness of the garden. The planning of the open garden on page 69 punctuates the space with a few carefully placed features and uses paving shapes to emphasize the width of the path. On page 76 there is another formal layout in which, although there are divisions, the full extent of the garden is visible along its central axis. The dramatic focal point of this long vista is the classic one of a statue backed by a dark hedge, but instead of laying a straight path heading directly towards this goal, the design interrupts the view with grass lawns and a pond with fountains.

The extreme dimensions of this long narrow garden are completely disguised by a design that uses abundant planting to hide the boundaries and divide the plot into separate compartments. Two elegant black glazed pots, one at the end of the paved area, the other at the end of an enclosed lawn, make elegant focal points. In the far corner an intriguing glimpse of a path reveals that the garden extends still further.

THE FAMILY GARDEN

This garden has been laid out in four distinct areas to suit a variety of family needs, but it has a very strong sense of movement, with one part flowing naturally into another. The mixture of formal geometrical elements and informal curving ones is successful because they are kept to separate areas. The path is the 'backbone' of the design, threading the different sections, styles and shapes together.

1 The main seating area is positioned obliquely to the rectangular axes of the garden, giving it a more interesting shape. The square paving, set on the diagonal, continues as the material for the path, becoming an attractive diamond pattern. To one side is a brick barbecue. Pots can be added for seasonal colour.

2 A fountain and pond, viewed across a small lawn, comprises the focal point of this first, relaxation area. The raised brick walls are wide enough for sitting, and the front one is stepped down so that more of the pond can be

seen when seated on the terrace. The rather rigid wall surround of the pond structure is softened by bold planting, including a small weeping tree such as *Salix caprea pendula* or *S. purpurea* 'Pendula'.

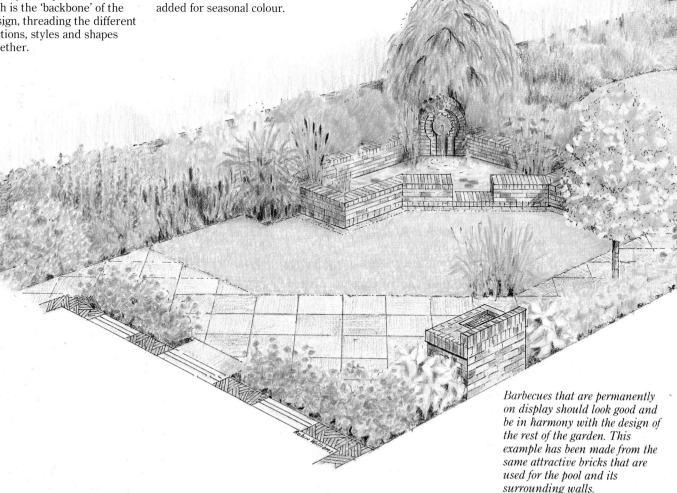

Barbecues that are permanently on display should look good and be in harmony with the design of the rest of the garden. This example has been made from the same attractive bricks that are used for the pool and its surrounding walls.

3 The path leads to a more informal plantsman's garden and soft lawn. It changes material, from paving to gravel, and shape – now winding round a tree and disappearing behind a curved bed – as the formal design merges with the informal.

4 A raised gazebo overlooks a children's play area and the climbing frame on the lawn is surrounded by tough child-resistant shrubs. Although functional, this area is designed to be attractive too, with four trees positioned at the corners, for balance and a pretty rose arch at the far end.

5 The formal vegetable garden is separated from the play area by an evergreen hedge; low hedging also edges the beds. Its symmetrical layout has a central focal point which, from the play area, is framed by the rose arch, at the entrance.

Above *Even the smallest water feature adds an extra dimension to a garden. As in the plan for the family garden on the previous pages, a brick-built pool set into a corner or against a wall makes the most of a narrow site. The design can exploit the height of the backdrop for plant interest, for a fountain, or (as here) by using a mirror to double the apparent extent of the water.*

Right *By offering a place to pause and rest, a seat offsets any sense that a narrow garden is a mere corridor. Backed by a hedge and flanked by symmetrical box-edged beds of hostas, this seat would make a terminal focal point or a quiet niche part-way along the garden's length.*

A formal garden

The prevailing atmosphere in this asymmetrical garden is one of calmness and simplicity, although the expanse of lawn is also good for children's games. The main seating area, which has a long seat overlooking a raised pool, is almost completely enclosed. From this separate 'room' the rest of the garden is hidden from view, but for a small gap in the dividing evergreen hedge. This affords a glimpse of a statue set against a further section of the hedge, shaded by an ornamental tree.

The path turns sharply round this tree and straightens to finish at the end of the garden. Formal borders edge the area. On one side, a bed with a large tree projects into the lawn, partly dividing the grassy area. Matching trees line the path, creating a long allée, with a seat providing a focal point at its end.

An informal garden

This garden is very simply divided in two. The far end is designed as a children's play area. It is a plain rectangle of grass with a single apple tree sheltering a seat.

In contrast, the larger section, nearer the house, is filled with beds, a circular seating area, a curving path and an oval lawn. Here the design deliberately goes against the rectangular lines imposed by the boundaries. The lawn is set askew, which ensures that the surrounding borders all have different shapes. The largest is 'landscaped', with low plants nearest the path and increasing in height up to a tall flowering tree. Another tree in the far corner shades a seat.

The hexagonal tiles on the seating area impart a static feeling but the winding path creates movement through the garden; it terminates in a focal point set against an evergreen backdrop. The hedge forms a visual barrier to the rear garden but is staggered, so providing a way through and giving a visual hint that the garden does continue.

An open garden

There are no separate compartments to this highly formal, symmetrical garden, and the prevailing atmosphere is one of openness, regularity and balance. Again there is plenty of space for children to run or cycle. From the terrace, with its formal patterned paving and symmetrical flower-filled planters, a path leads down the main axis. At its intersection with the cross axis is an intermediate focal point, such as a sundial, set on a circle of paving edged with low box hedges. On either side are ornamental stone seats.

From here the path is lined with six planted timber obelisks that lead to a clipped evergreen hedge surrounding a curved seat – the terminal focal point. On each side, two ornamental trees match those set further down the garden. Despite the length of the path it does not appear too narrow: the joints of the paving are deliberately staggered to give an impression of width, and the surrounding grass, too, adds to the broad open feeling.

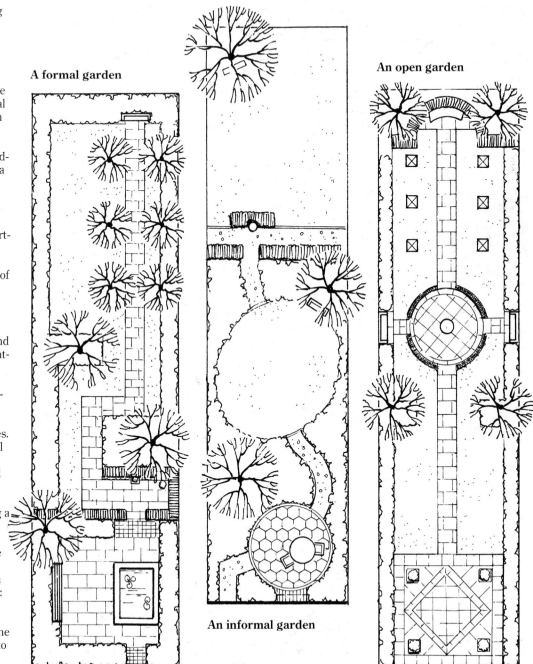

A formal garden

An open garden

An informal garden

THE SLOPING GARDEN

Wall fountains are very useful for providing the sight and sound of water when you don't wish to devote space to a pond. In this attractive terracotta example, the water is caught in the basin and returned to Pan's mouth by a tiny submersible pump via a pipe hidden behind the plaque.

Since this plot slopes downwards, its entire layout, despite its length, can be seen from the terrace next to the house and so it is important that it should look good as a whole. Here, the use of gentle curves invites a leisurely expansive look rather than drawing the eye straight down. The garden is shown here in its autumn colours.

The design creates three different areas, gradually changing in style and linked rather than compartmentalized. Slabs of natural stone are used throughout the garden, providing continuity, while fairly dense planting lends an air of softness.

1 The terrace forming the main seating area is quite spare and formal, with a pattern of bricks criss-crossing slabs of natural stone and a seat on one side balanced by a wall fountain on the other. Pots filled with annuals provide seasonal colour and, rather than a solid wall, the terrace is surrounded by wrought-iron railings providing a see-through safety barrier.

2 Broad stone steps curve gracefully down to the second level. They are bounded by stone walls topped with brick which, like the brick edges to the top two semi-circular steps, link with the patterning of the terrace. The curve partially encloses a raised bed filled with sun-loving plants. Its lower wall contains a niche into which is set a piece of sculpture, deliberately placed to be seen on the return journey through the garden.

3 A pergola, clad with an evergreen climber, such as ivy, shelters a seat overlooking a light expanse of lawn and flowerbed, punctuated at either end by two small specimen trees. In keeping with the more informal design of this part of the garden, the flat stone paving and steps here are no longer edged with brick.

4 A low stone seat is the terminal focal point of the garden as viewed from near the house. It is set in an area that is enclosed and shady, with lush informal planting. This has the feeling of a completely different world from the open, high, formal terrace, although the use of naturally shaped stone, running like a thread throughout the garden, strongly links both ends. The seat overlooks a small pond, edged and backed with natural stone, and, to the right, stone steps and a view back up the garden.

Above *Natural stone makes a perfect material for steps, harmonizing well with a variety of architectural and design moods. In an informal area, like the lower part of the garden on pages 70–71, stone steps seem part of the natural landscape, especially where a slope is designed as a rock garden; the smooth slabs contrast with the solid shapes of the rockery stones but preserve an overall unity.*

Right *This path threads its way at a leisurely pace through a gradually sloping garden (rather than moving the visitor briskly from one terrace to another). The broad treads enable you to pause comfortably and safely to appreciate the plants on either side, and the pattern of the setts does not compete for attention.*

A garden on different levels

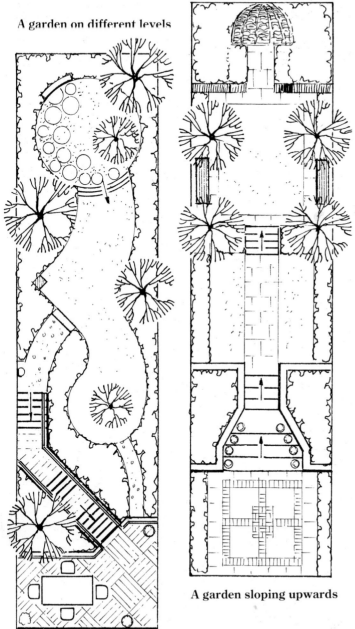

A garden sloping upwards

A garden on different levels

This design makes a feature of the differing levels of the sloping site by having a raised terrace of timber decking, thus exaggerating the difference in height from one end of the garden to the other. Timber steps and landings lead down to a gravel path and the central lawn. From here, the change in levels is again emphasized by the fact that the planting and gravel are seen to continue beneath and beyond the steps.

The shape of the lawn is largely determined by the trees – including the lawn specimen – around which it curves. A modern statue is set in a sharp 'corner', making it the focal point of the central area while remaining hidden from both ends.

Curved steps lead to the lowest part of the garden which – as in many sloping gardens – is rather damp. Moisture-loving plants surround a circular boggy area which is overlooked by a seat.

A garden sloping upwards

Here the plot has been divided into separate compartments and each has been given a strictly formal treatment. Changes in level hide the upper areas from the lower, but each has a symmetrical design that gives the garden a strong sense of direction, leading the visitor straight through to the end.

The brick-patterned patio next to the house is completely uncluttered, giving a feeling of space in what is really an enclosed area. Wide steps up add a sense of breadth to this narrow garden and are brightened and softened by planted pots on each tread.

The steps, bordered by raised beds for low-growing dry-loving plants, lead to the main flower garden, where a broad path through the lawn is surrounded by herbaceous plants and climbers. Further steps lead to an area for contemplation, with seats either side of a square lawn enclosed by four matched trees.

The end point of the garden journey is a charming summerhouse of woven willow or hazel, overgrown with roses and honeysuckle and surrounded by plants with bold foliage. Separated by a low evergreen hedge and path, it introduces a romantic feature to soften the garden.

THE VERY NARROW GARDEN

In a garden that is very narrow in comparison with its length the aim is to prevent its becoming a mere passageway. Here the garden has been divided into areas that are hidden from one another, using a soft yet highly formal style. It has also been designed to display a collection of sculpture. The pieces are given isolated settings so that they can be appreciated individually, and lights are placed to illuminate them – as well as to light the terrace – after dark. Tall evergreen hedges of yew or *Cupressus* give a strong structure to the garden; they need regular and careful clipping but, apart from this, the site is easily maintained.

1 The sunny terrace next to the house is the main seating area. Stone setts are laid in an attractive 'fishscale' pattern, a gentle formal style that is further softened if moss is allowed to colonize the joints. The terrace is furnished with a tiled table (useful both for *al fresco* meals and as a workbench), pots filled with bold-leaved plants, and timber planters containing shrubs grown as standard balls. To be structurally effective throughout the year these plants could be evergreens, such as box or bay, or, in warm climates, standard daisies such as *Argyranthemum frutescens.* Timber fences in a basket-weave pattern make an interesting and warm surround.

2 The path, too, is made from stone setts, this time laid in a geometrical pattern that both directs the visitor forwards by virtue of its strong lines and, together with a small step, visually separates it from the terrace. Hidden by a curved hedge and tree is the garden's first 'surprise' – a raised pool and sculptured fountain. Opposite is a simple bench seat.

3 The clipped hedge jutting out from the side contributes a maze-like feeling, making the path turn abruptly round it. On one side it backs a statue forming the terminal focal point of the path; back-to-back with this is a decorative Gothic-style chair that acts both as a resting place and a focal point on the return journey. From the chair can be seen a timber arch that forms the entrance to the furthest area and frames the view in both directions. The end of the hedge also acts as a foil to another piece of sculpture, completely hidden until the corner is turned.

4 The secret garden is almost entirely surrounded by a tall hedge and is a perfect area for peace and privacy. A simple seat looks across a soft green lawn of grass or other evergreen ground cover – paving here would look too cold – towards another piece of sculpture. On either side are planters that link thematically with the terrace.

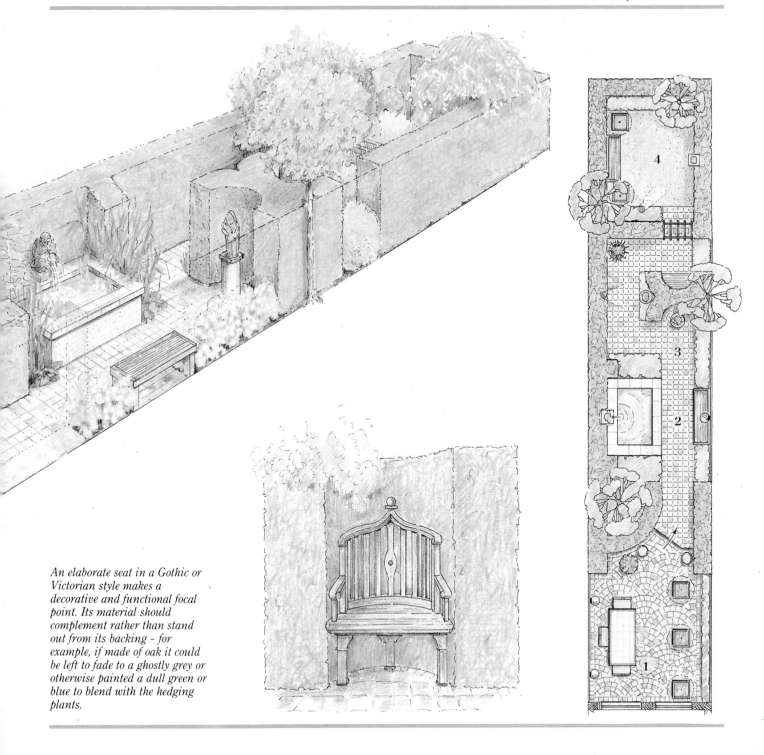

An elaborate seat in a Gothic or Victorian style makes a decorative and functional focal point. Its material should complement rather than stand out from its backing – for example, if made of oak it could be left to fade to a ghostly grey or otherwise painted a dull green or blue to blend with the hedging plants.

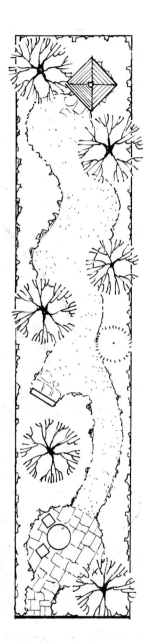

An informal garden

This simple, informal design treats the whole garden as one but uses gentle curves and strategically placed trees to stop the view at various points. Interest is created because from no point can the whole garden be seen.

The seating area near the house is laid with random natural stone and is circular, echoing the curving shape of the grass path as it winds round the garden's trees and shrubs. This path is the most important element in the garden, linking the different areas and acting as a backbone to the plan. It first curves round a winter-flowering tree – planted to look good from the house in winter – to a surprise: a hidden seat. This looks across to a conifer, planted so as to break up the fence, visually, especially in winter when its entire length is more obvious.

The grass then widens, giving the garden more breadth, and at the end repeats the circular shape of the main seating area. It is only on reaching this final part that the secret summerhouse is discovered, set back in a corner and shielded by trees either side.

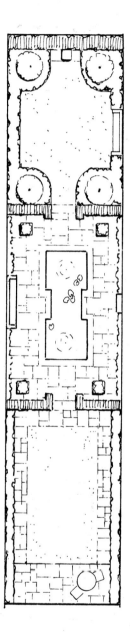

A garden of compartments

Here the strictly formal design allows a through view from one end of the garden to the other, emphasizing rather than disguising its length. However, division into three separate compartments and the placing of the pond and fountains in the centre prevents any impression of a passageway.

Nearest the house is an area for family activities, with a paved terrace for entertaining and a rectangular lawn for play. Colourful flowers and climbers grow in narrow beds each side.

The focal, light-reflecting point of the whole garden is the formal pond with a fountain at each end. It is an interesting hammer-head design – a long rectangle would over-emphasize the garden shape – and on one side of its thinnest part is a seat looking across it to a wall plaque on the other. This central area is entirely paved, apart from planting holes for wall climbers, and is separated from the others by tall clipped evergreen hedges. Matched planters, containing clipped box or bay trees, occupy the four corners and add to the formal air of symmetry.

The third area is just as symmetrically formal, but a carpet of grass and borders of aromatic shrubs and plants soften the atmosphere. A seat is positioned to be in shade when the one by the pond is in sun (and vice versa). At the end, backed by a dark hedge, is a statue forming the garden's terminal focal point – a highly important and dramatic position since, from the other end, it is reflected in the water.

This long narrow plot is divided into separate compartments, like the formal garden opposite, in the manner of a grand formal walk. Each area has its own symmetrical plan and works on a more intimate scale that can be appreciated comfortably. The straight line of the path is interrupted, first by a paved circle which visually pushes out the parallel hedges and makes the garden seem wider, then by a stone fountain which the path must circumnavigate.

Although the layout is formal, the use of curving and rounded forms in the planting and topiary (and particularly the low, fat bushes of golden box) softens its severity. Even the mauve heads of the alliums seem to sustain the theme of plant spheres.

LARGE RECTANGULAR GARDENS

There is plenty of scope for dividing a large rectangular garden into smaller units, and this is the best way of avoiding a too open, playing-field-like atmosphere. The divisions can vary from physically enclosed areas for special purposes – growing vegetables and fruit, accommodating children's ball games or siting a swimming pool – to the more loosely separated areas of an informal ornamental garden.

You can base the design on an open central area with a spacious expanse of grass or water, either formal or informal. You can choose a formal, geometric layout such as the dramatic panel of water in the garden on pages 84–5 or the Moorish-style pool on page 87. However, plenty of space means the possibility of opting for an informal, natural atmosphere even in a built-up area, with dense planting of trees and shrubs to obscure man-made boundaries and screen out neighbours. The designs on pages 88–91 demonstrate the careful thinking behind a garden that seems to have evolved naturally.

In a large garden, it will often be possible to offer a choice of sitting areas in sun or shade. Plants, too, will appreciate the natural benefits of different parts of the site. Tender plants will flourish in a particularly sheltered corner or against a sunny wall while, not far away, shade-loving plants can enjoy the canopy of a few shrubs and trees making a miniature woodland. An open area away from trees will be ideal for siting a pond, surrounded by moisture-loving marginal plants. You may want to segregate different colour schemes or planting themes; herbs and roses are subjects that often merit gardens-within-a-garden.

Dividing the garden

You can separate areas with fencing, trellis or formal planting – a dense hedge, a more open mesh of espalier fruit trees, or a rose-entwined pergola – but suggestion can be as useful as purely physical barriers. You can plant shrubs and trees in an informal way to provide the necessary screening, suggesting that the visitor is passing from one garden area to another. A lawn like the one in the informal garden on page 83 that is 'waisted', curving in and then out where borders project on either side, instantly creates an impression of two separate but interconnected garden areas. Paradoxically, encroaching on the lawn in this way visually extends the garden, since it is not all visible at once, and the hidden corners are an inducement to explore.

You can also create garden divisions by exploiting natural changes in ground level, or introducing them with the use of raised areas such as decking. Other ground-level devices that signal a change of garden 'zone' include a deliberate shift from manicured lawn to grass that is kept less closely mown. A band of longer grass – perhaps sprinkled with naturalized bulbs – makes a good link between the formal garden and freer shrub planting or even a 'wild' area.

You need to be careful not to destroy the overall unity of a large garden by making it too fragmented. You can use similar planting or materials in different parts of the garden. Paths can provide the aesthetic as well as the physical link between separate areas by being made in the same design or material. The larger the garden, the more important it is to have some unifying guidelines – visual ones to help you appreciate the lines of the composition, and practical ones underfoot to lead you round it.

Areas of different plant interest subdivide a large expanse of garden in an informal way. This plot has the benefit of a stream, which sets the keynote for naturalistic plantings of moisture-loving species along its margins. The winding path and the bridge create firm shapes on the ground plan, and the generous expanse of open lawn balances the massed planting at the waterside. A group of solid-looking evergreens adds weight to the composition.

THE FAMILY GARDEN

The length of this garden is almost twice its width and its main axis runs from top to bottom. The plot narrows towards the end and is typical of many that correspond with a curve in the road. The shape of the central grassed area gives breadth to the garden, its generous curves increasing the sense of space. The path is the key element in linking the various garden areas together. It contributes to the general atmosphere of tranquillity, with changing views as the visitor progresses from one area to another.

1 The main terrace is approached by a step down from the house and the bricks bordering it provide a strong design link with the house. Its lines harmonize with the lawn and the surface is of natural paving stones laid in a random pattern, defined by the edging of regular brickwork. It is wide and provides a spacious area for relaxing and entertaining. At the side, a barbecue sits against a raised bed which, together with the materials used, helps it blend in with the rest of the garden. When sitting on the terrace there are two focal points – immediately ahead lies the pond and to the left a vase or figure nestles among foliage plants.

2 The path wends its way from one seating area to another, following the soft curves of the lawn. Twin trees, such as *Robinia pseudoacacia*, near the terrace form a natural gateway. A break in the border allows a clear view back to the house and the path then passes through a shady, enclosed area and round to the ornamental pond. Here a bench offers an immediate view of the pool.

This is sunny when the main terrace is in shade and vice versa. The path extension to the unobtrusively positioned garden shed eases the access for machinery.

3 The lawn enhances the width of the garden through the careful use of curves. It is surrounded by trees and mixed beds of herbaceous plants and shrubs. A large evergreen shrub is positioned to act as a screen for the garden shed and a raised planter next to the terrace softens the change from the border to the hard brick surface.

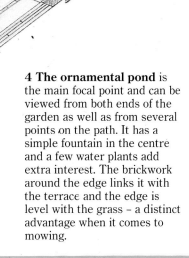

4 The ornamental pond is the main focal point and can be viewed from both ends of the garden as well as from several points on the path. It has a simple fountain in the centre and a few water plants add extra interest. The brickwork around the edge links it with the terrace and the edge is level with the grass – a distinct advantage when it comes to mowing.

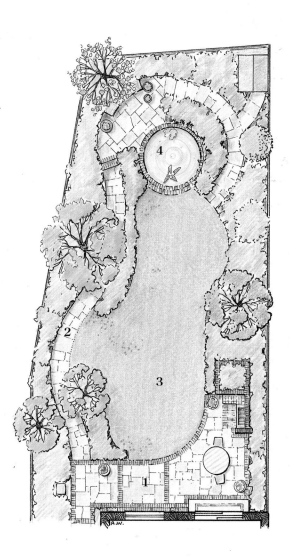

Gravel makes a good alternative to lawn, as in the plan for the low-maintenance garden below. As with grass, its smooth expanse can be given shape and interest by punctuating stepping stones which lead the eye and the feet in the direction the designer intends. Gravel also has the advantage over grass of looking good in more abstract modern designs. As a foil to plants such as grasses and bamboos, gravel will conjure a distinctly oriental atmosphere.

A low-maintenance garden
This treatment of a large rectangular plot is similar to the family garden on pages 80–81, but the focal point has been significantly altered by removing the ornamental pond and turning the terrace into a circular area, encroaching into the central space. Rocks and gravel replace the lawn, considerably decreasing the amount of time needed to maintain the garden. Gravel is always a labour-saving surface as weeds can easily be removed. The second, smaller, seating area provides a shady corner and an alternative view.

Mixed borders surround and enclose most of the main terrace, while the opening at the front allows the eye to be led towards the end of the garden, now dominated by a large tree and several shrubs.

The now extended paths leading to the smaller terrace are part of the labour-saving solution. The two paths are made of different surfaces, paving slabs and gravel.

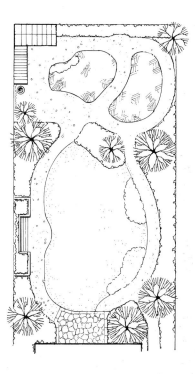

An easy-access garden

This garden with its regular shapes has been designed for easy access by a wheelchair. The key element once again is the flat path, made from self-binding gravel which produces a firm compacted surface. Since sharp corners are awkward for wheels, the path traverses the entire plot in gentle curves, imposing a soft informal structure on the garden.

From the natural stone patio the path leads up one side of the large open lawn. Half-way along is a raised bed enclosing a seat. Here the path widens, making a semi-circular area, echoing the curves of the lawn edge opposite, that is wide enough to accommodate several people – including the wheelchair-bound – pausing here.

The path continues through a plantation of shrubs and trees that screens the vegetable garden. This area contains a greenhouse and store, fruit, cut flowers and herbs as well as vegetables, and is criss-crossed by the path. Returning to the house, beds planted with tall shrubs hide the lawn from the path, creating a series of 'windows' through which to glimpse a view.

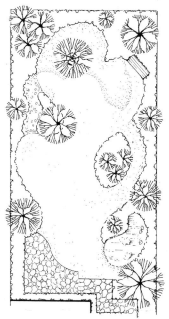

An informal garden

The regular rectangular shape of this plot is disguised by the use of free-flowing shapes. Although the main area is a large expanse of lawn, its borders are seen to curve quite dramatically, narrowing and expanding at various points, and from any position there are always some hidden areas.

In a near corner a large natural stone patio with a flowing edge overlooks the lawn and the pond. Curving into the shrub border, the pond appears in different shapes depending on the viewing point and can seldom be seen in its entirety. Further up the garden, peat or bark-chip paths wind through areas hidden by beds planted with trees and shrubs. At the far end is a more natural, wilder area, where the grass is less frequently mown and blends easily into the surrounding borders.

THE WATER GARDEN

Where water is the central element in a garden it generally creates an atmosphere of peace and tranquillity, and this is certainly true here. The overall design is very strong and formal, using clean lines and clear geometric shapes, and yet the garden is light, open and delicate. The design also adds interest by providing distinct areas giving very different 'pictures' of the garden. A circular *motif* is repeated throughout and, together with a continuity in the use of materials for paving and walls, brings a sense of unity to the garden.

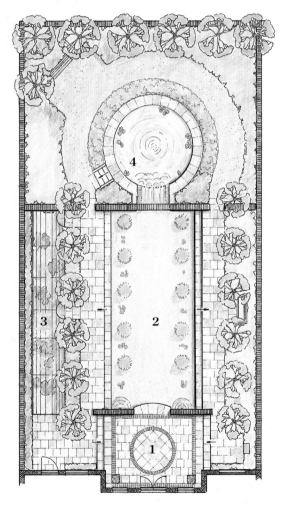

1 The terrace next to the house provides the main seating area. It is paved with brick and regular stone slabs and incorporates a brick circle. On either side, steps lead down to a paved lower level and, to the right, a bust on a pedestal makes a secondary focal point, balancing the cross view. The main view overlooks the pool, and the walls at the end of the terrace have been deliberately designed so that their shape both directs the eye down the pool and frames this view.

2 The rectangular pool is formal and balanced; hidden from the terrace, two wall fountains trickle water in a measured flow, and even the water plants have been placed symmetrically. On either side is a wide paved path, and steps down lead the paving right to the water's edge. Lining the paths are symmetrically planted small trees framing the pool area. At the end water flows through the graceful shape of a Moon window, set in a brick wall. This striking focal point both holds the eye and frames the area beyond.

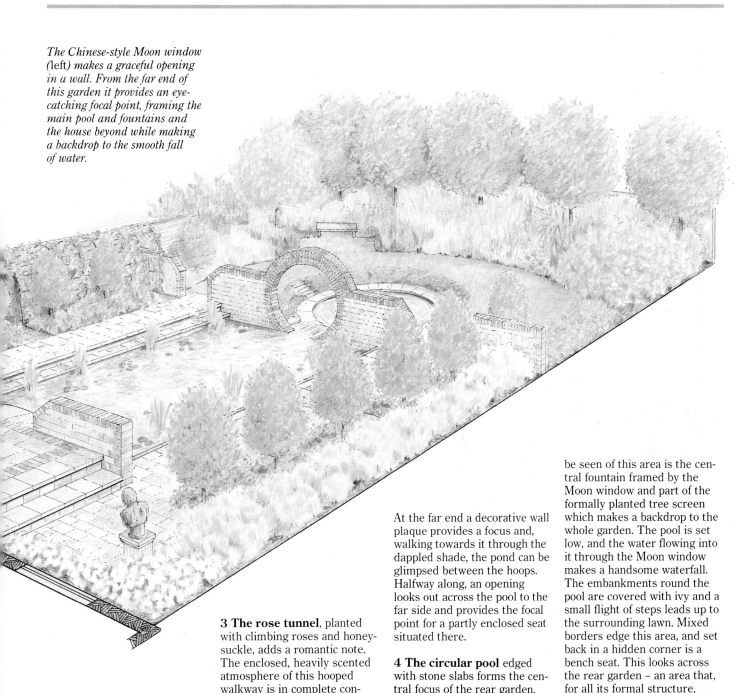

The Chinese-style Moon window (left) makes a graceful opening in a wall. From the far end of this garden it provides an eye-catching focal point, framing the main pool and fountains and the house beyond while making a backdrop to the smooth fall of water.

3 The rose tunnel, planted with climbing roses and honeysuckle, adds a romantic note. The enclosed, heavily scented atmosphere of this hooped walkway is in complete contrast to the rest of the garden.

At the far end a decorative wall plaque provides a focus and, walking towards it through the dappled shade, the pond can be glimpsed between the hoops. Halfway along, an opening looks out across the pool to the far side and provides the focal point for a partly enclosed seat situated there.

4 The circular pool edged with stone slabs forms the central focus of the rear garden. From the terrace all that can be seen of this area is the central fountain framed by the Moon window and part of the formally planted tree screen which makes a backdrop to the whole garden. The pool is set low, and the water flowing into it through the Moon window makes a handsome waterfall. The embankments round the pool are covered with ivy and a small flight of steps leads up to the surrounding lawn. Mixed borders edge this area, and set back in a hidden corner is a bench seat. This looks across the rear garden – an area that, for all its formal structure, creates an informal picture.

Timber decking seems to have a natural affinity with water features. It is useful too, for disguising the tell-tale edges of artificial pools made with plastic liners. It is the ideal material for bridges – either real ones spanning a stretch of water, or mock bridges separating the real pool from a patch of low-set waterside plants that make it look bigger than it actually is. The clean lines of the regularly spaced boards look good in modern settings and make an ideal foil for plants and planted containers. Designs are easily adaptable to gardens large and small.

As shown here, exciting angles and changes of level look most attractive. They can also be exploited to make a feature that contrasts with the outline of a regularly shaped plot, as in the design shown opposite.

A deck garden

This slightly squarer site has been laid out so that all lines run obliquely to the plot. This takes advantage of the long diagonal axes and makes the view from the house more interesting than if the timber walkways ran parallel to the sides. The asymmetrically formal design uses straight lines everywhere, with timber decking for all hard surfaces.

Substantial planting of bold-leaved trees and shrubs associates well with the rectilinear shapes of the decking and pond and disguises the potentially awkward-looking corners created by the oblique layout. Where a corner would project unattractively into the deck area nearest the house it has simply been blunted.

The water is edged with simple block or brickwork which is hidden or softened by marginal planting. Visually the pond appears in three parts, with the small section nearest the house divided from the main pool by a raised timber walkway; posts on either side – part of the supporting structure – can be linked by ropes for safety. The farthest section, hidden from much of the garden, is on a higher level, with a fountain at its head and a waterfall at its foot.

There are three seating areas, each different in character and outlook. One is hidden away in the near right-hand corner and looks towards the fountain and waterfall. In a far corner an open-sided, covered summerhouse forms the main focal point of the garden and provides shady seating. It looks down the main expanse of water ahead and, near it to the left, overlooks a small square bed devoted to bog plants. The main seating area is a spacious, sunny square of decking near the house, with a wide view of the garden, on which table and chairs are set.

An informal garden

In this natural-looking design expanses of grass and water are almost woven together. No hard lines are used, and even the permanently dry seating area next to the house is made of natural stone set in grass to give a soft effect. The main lawn area gradually divides into two grass paths that curve round and, linked by a slatted timber bridge, cross over the large pond. In shady or damp areas there are winding paths of gravel or peat.

From the lawn the one large expanse of water appears as two as it bends out of sight. Moisture-loving plants and trees are planted at its margins and corner-like edges are softened by the creation of small beaches of broken local stone or pebbles. The 'prize' for venturing along the maze of paths is the discovery of a summerhouse tucked away in a corner. Hexagonal in shape, it partly projects over the water, creating shadows on the surface.

A deck garden

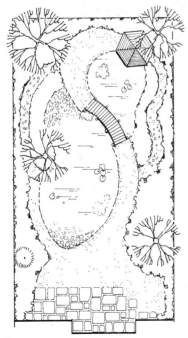

An informal garden

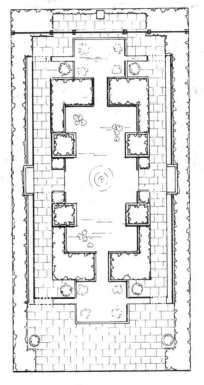

A Moorish garden

A Moorish garden

The design of this strictly formal, symmetrical garden deliberately re-creates the feeling of Moorish gardens in Spain, and would be particularly effective in a hot climate or a sunny position. A canal linked to the main pool runs round the edges of the garden, under paths and under seats and so gives the magical impression of being surrounded by water.

The main seating area next to the house is laid with rectangular paving slabs that form the hard surface throughout the garden. Halfway along the paths either side of the pool are two seats facing each other and overlooking the central fountain; the canal passes beneath them.

Although the pool is a regular shape, views of it are made interesting by the way beds and planters make it narrow and widen. The four square planters are slightly raised above the water level and are planted with low shrubs such as prostrate cotoneasters and junipers that spill over the edges, making fascinating shapes and mysterious corners. The nearest and farthest beds contain plants with spiky foliage, such as irises, which frame the pool beyond. Moving round the garden, the view of the water constantly opens and closes.

At the far end a statue forms the terminal focal point and is atmospherically reflected in the far pool. A single beam supported by posts makes a light open pergola for a climbing rose or wisteria, and frames the statue.

THE NATURAL GARDEN

Apart from the degree of planning that is evident near the house, this garden looks as if it has evolved naturally – and indeed it has been designed so to appear. In fact it has a firm structure that both disguises the rectangular shape and creates a sense of movement through the garden, and is deliberately filled with plants and features that are wild or natural-looking and that will attract wildlife to the garden. Wattle fencing and heavy planting at the periphery help obscure the artificial boundaries, contributing to the natural look.

1 A natural stone path, set in grass, leads from the main doors to a slightly raised circular seating area of grass edged with stone, with a timber seat at one side. This is surrounded by tall planting and is hidden from most of the garden and so does not detract from the semi-wild feel of the design.

2 The central meadow is sown with wildflower and grass seed appropriate to the soil type and aspect, and infrequently mown. Its curving shape, determined by the contours of the surrounding beds, creates secluded corners and enticing glimpses of further half-hidden areas. In several such corners, timber bench seats are placed to give a series of private views, each completely different. Edges of the meadow are closely mown to create paths for easier walking.

3 A pond positioned in the most open area of the garden makes a perfect home and watering hole for a wide variety of animal, bird and insect life, and serves as a charming focal point for the garden. Boggy plants and diminutive forms of otherwise invasive water plants, such as water iris and bulrush, are planted at the margins and the edges, forming a natural-looking surround.

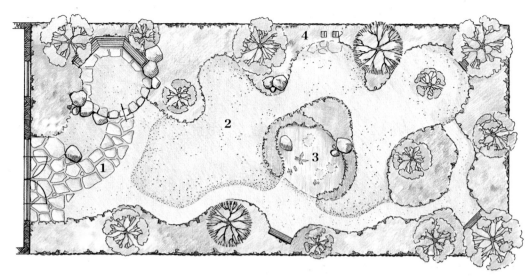

4 Bee hives carefully situated in a little clearing by the border reveal this to be the garden of a dedicated wildlife enthusiast, since hives need skilled attention. The borders themselves are stocked with trees, shrubs and flowers that provide food and pollen for all kinds of wildlife. They are encouraged to grow in natural-looking profusion to provide shelter.

Woven material such as hazel or willow makes the best sort of fencing for a natural garden, providing an appropriate backdrop and a host for climbers. Wattle fencing also makes a good barrier, gently filtering the wind.

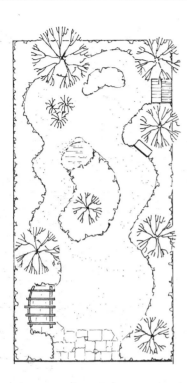

A garden with open spaces

This solution is for a family that wants a fairly wild garden but needs open space for play and other family activities. Although showing similarities to the garden on pages 88–9, the layout is simpler. However, the curves of the border and the central island bed assure that there are always hidden areas screened from view, and the planting is natural-looking and intended to attract wildlife.

Natural stone forms an open seating area next to the house and also a path leading to a wooden arbor covered with honeysuckle. Both of these overlook an open expanse of lawn, which runs away, enticingly, in two directions on either side of the island bed that hides the end of the garden. The grass, especially at the far end, is not tightly mown, and wildflowers are encouraged to grow.

On the right-hand side a border containing a tall tree, and jutting out into the lawn space, encloses a seat and hides a garden shed. From one side of the seat the view goes back to the house; the other looks toward a small pond at the end of the central bed. The curving shapes of lawn and beds look natural and invite movement through the garden.

A garden meeting two needs

This design meets the contrasting needs of a family that wants a fairly natural garden but with an element of formality and space for a large, regular-shaped swimming pool. The answer here is to divide the garden in two.

At the far end, the oval swimming pool is laid diagonally to maximize its length. At one end, a curved wooden seat overlooks the pool and, on the far side, a low building houses a changing room and heating and filtration units. The color of the pool's lining helps integrate it with the naturally planted border – a dark color for temperate climates, with light blue or turquoise appropriate only for hot sunny climates.

The material excavated when making the pool has been used to raise this area, and this in effect hides the pool from the rest of the garden. From the terrace next to the house, all that can be seen is the retaining wall and curved steps up, and the planting in the beds surrounding the pool. This means that the more natural atmosphere of the first area is not spoiled, and there is no feeling of foreshortening (since the trees and shrubs at the far end can be seen).

Next to the house the large formally paved seating area curves gently out into a lawn which, though fairly neat, is not so closely mown as to eliminate wildflowers. The surrounding beds too, though fairly neatly shaped, contain a profusion of wildflowers, trees and shrubs planted to attract birds and wildlife. A seat is tucked into a curving border and backed by an evergreen tree to provide shade. A specimen tree in the lawn makes a focal point for both seating areas, with the grass winding intriguingly behind it.

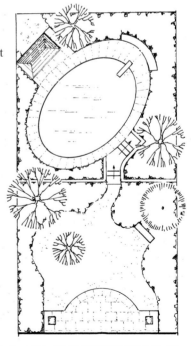

In this garden, designed to be filled with natural planting and as a home for wildlife, a strong structure holds it all together without detracting from its informal atmosphere.

A pond, well situated in an open area and surrounded by natural waterside planting, gives a bright focus to the garden and provides a great attraction for wildlife. Behind, a mown grass path cuts through a wildflower meadow and leads intriguingly through to a sheltering cluster of trees. A daisy-covered lawn, allowed to grow fairly long rather than 'manicured', gently encloses beds planted in profusion with wild and cottage-garden flowers. The beds are given a firm shape with well-defined, though not neat, edges.

TRIANGULAR GARDENS

Triangular sites occur more frequently than might be expected. They are often found when a house has been built beside an existing barrier such as a curving road, or when a site borders some natural landscape feature such as water. In such cases one side of the garden might have an irregular free-flowing line following that of the physical barrier, while the other two represent the straight legal demarcations of the plot. Sometimes two of the sides are irregular – perhaps when the site has been shaped by boundaries of an earlier, less regimented age, such as old hedges.

The triangular garden is not the easiest plot to design. Whether the shape is geometric or free-flowing it can seem limited and awkwardly angled. The far end of a triangular area draws the eye strongly, because the boundaries converge quickly to form an apex. You will notice this particularly in the stark expanse of a new garden, where no existing features mask the effect by distracting the attention from the shape and newly erected fences or walls emphasize the lines of the boundary.

Changing the proportions

You cannot of course, physically change the uncomfortable convergence of triangular boundaries. However, you can change the appearance of the garden, especially by how you arrange the vertical elements of the plan in relation to the boundaries. You can place features such as trees so that they arrest movement or increase it. You can even use false perspective to correct or disguise the proportions, perhaps by exaggerating the distance of a corner, creating an illusion of almost infinite space where the plot narrows to a point. The gradual narrowing of the grass path in the formal 'specialist' garden on page 97, which terminates in a building that is subtly undersized, is a perfect example of stretching the visual limits. (In this garden, a screening pair of trees and containers divide the view and counteract the uncomfortable corridor sensation of such strong directional movement.)

If you use the vertical elements in the garden to change the proportions and provide an alternative sense of movement you will need to balance the design with areas of tranquillity. Any patterning in paving or stonework in the foreground should fit in with the effects you are trying to achieve. In any triangular area, it is a good idea for the ground-plan to be based around a stable shape such as an expanse of lawn or paving that draws the attention back from the perimeters. Static formal shapes, like the octagons used in the family garden on pages 94–5 or the circles of the seaside garden on pages 98–9, answer this need perfectly.

You can also use planting to disguise the converging lines of the boundaries, as a number of the following designs do, so that the shape of the garden is no longer evident. The odd awkward corners can provide hidden benefits and be the making of an intriguing garden. They are ideal places to tuck away out of sight such necessities as sheds and compost heaps. As in the garden on page 94–5, you could use them to enshrine some secret focal point – a special piece of sculpture, perhaps – reached by a winding route through shrubs, and providing a reward for those who have journeyed to it.

This spacious open design uses a severe geometry of angles to create such a strong ground plan that attention is drawn away from the overall triangular shape of the plot. The open area is subdivided into satisfying expanses of lawn, stone paving and brick – the last two contrasting in the scale of their patterning but harmonizing in tone. Subtle changes in level further enhance the interest of this horizontal plane. Complementing the fine proportions of the design, and balancing its slight austerity, are the colours and textures of a generous herbaceous border, with plants spilling over and breaking up its straight edge. The foliage of trees, shrubs and climbers further softens and disguises the boundaries.

THE FAMILY GARDEN

In this design the triangular shape of the garden has been disguised, partly by obscuring the boundaries – especially at the apex – with full planting, and partly by basing the ground plan on a series of linked octagons, focusing attention inwards away from the narrowing boundary lines. The octagon – a formal alternative to the circle – is a wide static shape that gives a sense of space. The clear lines and materials used give this garden a light modern feel.

1 The seating area is octagonal and paved with a textured buff-coloured concrete, which increases the sense of stillness here since there are no paving joint lines that suggest movement or direction. This material is used throughout the garden for continuity. A raised border filled with scented plants encloses one side and a long concrete seat is set against it. Another similarly planted raised bed balances the arrangement and helps enclose the whole area.

2 The octagonal lawn is a step down from the rest of the garden. It makes a good play space for young children and its low surrounding wall provides seating. On one side a path gently rises towards the boundary and then turns behind a bed of shrubs and a small tree. Balancing this cross axis, is a tree in a corner of the border which juts out and encloses a small statue that makes a focal point from the far end of the garden.

3 The pool and fountain provide the main prospect when looking towards the far end, its long canal adding to the impression of the garden's length. While the children are young it can be filled with pebbles almost to the surface so that the water is shallow enough to be safe. A geometrically shaped higher lawn surrounds the pool and fountain and leads back to the house.

4 A path winds out of sight from the upper lawn through the far end of the garden, which is heavily planted to disguise its pointed shape. At its end is a reward for making the journey – a piece of sculpture, hidden from the main part of the garden so as not to clash with the focal point formed by the pool and fountain.

The steps and wall coping show how textured concrete, used imaginatively as in this garden, can be an attractive and versatile material. They are constructed of poured concrete that has had the aggregate – gravel or pebbles – exposed by gentle washing and brushing just before hardening.

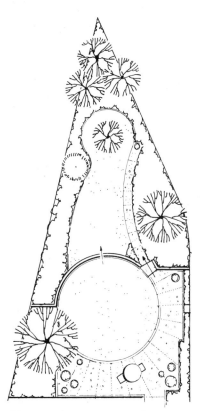

A low-maintenance garden

A low-maintenance garden
Circular shapes, rather than the harder-edged octagons of the design on pages 94–5, form the underlying structure of this scheme, again disguising the triangular shape. Curving borders filled with low-maintenance shrubs obscure the converging boundaries, with trees on each side providing the natural rationale for the curves and a cluster of trees hiding the pointed end.

The central lawn is partly surrounded by the extensive seating area of easy-care textured concrete, which is decorated with radiating joint lines and brightened by various pots and planters. Steps lead up to a path that curves round a border, with a boldly planted pot providing a terminating point. The upper lawn contains a weeping tree at the centre of its circular end; this is the garden's main focal point.

As in the low-maintenance garden above, a lawn on two levels adds interest to the ground plan without breaking its continuity. A static shape like a circle – often a recurring design theme – holds the eye, distracting attention from awkward corners. Here the brick-edged semicircle of grass acts like an anchor, stabilizing the more free-flowing expanse of the lower lawn. Imagine this picture without the 'step' device. The rich planting would still speak for itself, but the overall design would lack its note of distinction.

A specialist garden
This is a garden for a family who also have an interest in a particular shrub or flower type and want these plants displayed prominently. The formal design deliberately emphasizes the triangular shape of the plot and even manipulates it by employing false perspective. The central grass path narrows along its length, giving the impression of extra distance and bringing with it a strong sense of movement. At its end a gazebo or summerhouse – slightly smaller than normal to preserve the visual lie – provides the main focal point (and hides a storage area).

Beds for the specialized planting line the path. Behind them are borders where taller shrubs serve as a foil for the special plants and provide interest when they are not in season. Matching trees and planters divide the garden halfway down and prevent it being corridor-like. The curved terrace projects into a semicircular area of lawn, providing a spacious place for seating and recreation.

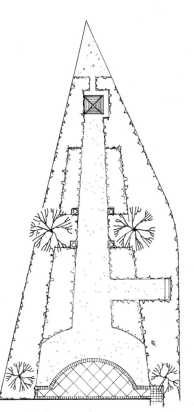

A specialist garden

THE SEASIDE GARDEN

The main drawback of a sea-side garden – the continual, and at times severe, salt-laden wind – is commonly balanced by the advantage of relatively mild winters (frosts are fewer near the sea) and often by the possession of a spectacular view. In this garden, careful design and planting create a sheltered environment with a sea view and plenty of space for family activities.

Surrounding the garden is a screening evergreen hedge that filters the wind, rather than stopping it and creating turbulence on the 'sheltered' side. A gap, filled by a post and rail fence, affords a good view over the water. The borders are filled with colourful salt-resistant plants, shrubs and trees whose taller members will grow in fantastic shapes sculpted by the prevailing winds. The whole layout is designed around bold and informal curves and circles, disguising the triangular shape.

1 The terrace next to the house is laid with regular paving slabs and decorated with smooth beach pebbles. It provides a generous area for seating and for play after wet weather. On the left side it becomes a path, with steps, to the sunken lawn. At the back, four beams set into flower beds support a pergola for climbing roses against the house-wall. From the terrace the main view looks towards the sea, clearly seen through the gap in the hedge.

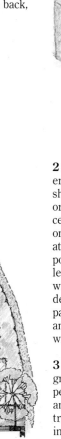

2 The circular lawn is deliberately set down to provide a sheltered area in which to sit or play on breezy days. At its centre is an armillary sphere on a pedestal that makes an attractive and fitting focal point. A gentle embankment leads up to the main lawn, whose interesting shape – determined by borders and path – is large enough to lend an air of spaciousness to the whole garden.

3 A path of self-binding gravel, again edged with beach pebbles, leads from the terrace and winds invitingly round the trees and out of sight. It ends in a sheltered intimate area centering on a circular summerhouse-cum-children's playhouse – an excellent vantage point for looking out to sea. Tall trees bear the brunt of the wind in this corner. The surrounding area is paved with natural local stone; small rockery groups are planted with smaller annuals and carpeting plants. The summerhouse is the main focal point from the opposite side of the garden, but is partially screened from the terrace so as not to conflict with the main view of the sea.

The round shape of the strongly built summerhouse is one that best withstands strong winds. The building is double glazed against draught, rain and cold, making it a warm place to sit, even in winter. It is also ideally placed for imaginative games of sailing ships.

A weekend garden

Many seaside gardens are attached to houses used infrequently or at weekends, and this is an informal, low-maintenance design for such a situation. Most of the plot is covered with easily maintained hard surfaces, with only two narrow beds in which are planted hardy climbers that cover a simple pergola. The pergola shelters a curving walkway that links a rectangular terrace next to the house to a circular seating area in the sheltered narrow corner overlooking the sea.

Terrace, path and seating area are paved with randomly laid rectangular stone. The surface of the main central area is shingle dotted with slabs that match the paving.

Through the shingle grow seaside plants and, apart from occasional weeding, these can be left to themselves. Hedging plants, such as tamarisk that looks best when left to grow informally, surround and, together with a few trees, shelter the plot.

The shape of the garden is not disguised and indeed has been echoed in the internal structure. The path follows the contour of the curved side and, on the opposite edge, three matching blossom trees interspersed with pots are placed in a regular line, drawing the eye towards the far corner. However, attention is also focused on the centre of the garden, where a small circular pond is edged with stone, and a curved stone block provides a seat.

Above *While the summerhouse in the seaside garden on the previous pages is solidly built for all-year use, in an inland garden the design can be more purely decorative. This open-sided hexagonal structure offers shelter from sun rather than wind or rain and its rustic simplicity suits the context of a country garden. Its main role is that of an architectural ornament, creating a strong and dramatic focal point in a fairly informal layout. The ground pattern of gravel and paving underlines this design function.*

Right *Like a terrace or patio, a pergola can exploit the transitional area which is neither house nor garden, neither indoors nor out. On one hand, the regular architectural structure can be seen as an extension of the building; this structure might not be appropriate in more naturally planted areas or more awkwardly contoured parts of the plot. On the other, the drapery of climbing plants links the structure to the garden. In the plan on the previous pages the pergola is set against the house wall in this way. In the plan for a weekend garden (above left) a freestanding pergola sheltering a path follows the curve of the boundary, creating a vertical design element in its own right.*

WIDE SHALLOW GARDENS

Gardens that are wide and shallow can be relatively awkward to deal with. Those at the rear of the house tend to lack depth and dimension; those at the front are often additionally sectioned off in various ways by essential paths and driveways.

It seems that many gardens depend for their success on a sense of space and distance, which is just what is lacking in a garden that is wider than it is deep. However, you can compensate for this. You can create the illusion of perspective deliberately by all sorts of visual tricks. A high wall or fence at the rear of the garden can masquerade as an internal garden division, implying that this is just the first of many successive compartments. A design like the one on pages 104–105 makes the rear backdrop interesting with a series of archways, one of which is a false gateway backed with mirror. The arch is an economical device for suggesting depth.

You can emphasize the short axis of the garden, geometrically, with a straight path, as in the formal garden on page 106. You can plant trees to provide a pattern or a focus that distracts from the shallow shape or, in more informal groupings, may actually hide the boundaries from view. As well as adjusting perspective with formal geometry, you can choose appropriate colours to help counteract the foreshortened effect. Avoid planting eye-catching yellow and red, which reduce the apparent distance. Misty, pale colours – particularly blues – always seem further away. On the ground, you can extend the space by expanses of pale-toned paving or gravel and light-reflecting water.

In all the garden designs shown, a strong internal ground plan based on curves and circles pushes out the parallel boundaries and breaks up the rectangle. These shapes focus attention away from the perimeters. The sense of movement of these curves makes a closed circuit which is satisfying in itself: it is not (as in more complex designs) aimed to prompt wanderings in search of hidden garden secrets.

Front gardens

Front gardens are the public setting for a house – indeed they may not even have the strong demarcation lines of hedges or fences, and are often designed just as a stretch of lawn, continuous with those of one's neighbours. However, if you do want a semi-private space, it will need to look good from both the house and the road – preferably reflecting or complementing the style of the house – and to provide clear access.

Curving lines and strong circular motifs are an equally good basis for designs in front gardens, where the overall shape is often more fragmented. Access to the front door may leave you with two or more asymmetrical or awkwardly shaped panels of ornamental garden and you might have to give priority to a driveway, garage or car-parking space rather than to planting. However, with careful planning, your front garden can look like a garden rather than a car park. Choice of attractive 'hard' elements contributes considerably to the success of a design: the paving of the driveway in the garden shown on pages 108–9 makes this large area a positive feature rather than a wasted space.

You can create unity between awkward, 'left-over' shapes or disparate elements not only with edging materials but also with a linking planting theme. If the proportions are good, attractive planting will enhance them, and masses of low-key greenery offer a useful disguise for oddly shaped patches. A carpeting of evergreen ground cover, for instance, is a muted background against which a well-placed container of seasonal planting makes a brilliant focal point.

The bold design of this shallow front garden focuses attention on the elegant central parterre, composed of standard roses, and edging and spirals of box, lined with Lonicera nitida *'Baggesen's Gold'. The garden's formal layout is softened by the planting: the centrepiece is not neatly clipped and the boundaries are disguised by shrubs and climbers grown in lush informality.*

THE FAMILY GARDEN

In this garden a dramatic internal structure focusing attention inwards and an element of *trompe l'oeil* along the back wall disguise the lack of depth. The ground plan is so handsome that it can almost be appreciated better from a position of height, making it a perfect garden for a tall town house. Although the layout is formal, curves rather than straight lines are used everywhere, and the design is further softened by the pastel-hued planting – predominantly of blue, pink and white.

1 Natural stone paving is used for the small seating area outside the house doors and for the path, which curves round one side to the back of the garden and ends by turning back to the lawn. It consists of large and small pieces of stone, roughly circular in shape. This shape is repeated throughout the garden, giving a strong sense of movement.

2 A low box hedge curves round in a bold flowing line to frame and form the lawn shape. This internal figure is made more dramatic because it contrasts so strongly with the rectangular shape of the plot, although the surrounding beds have been filled with trees and other planting that softens the corners to prevent the contrast becoming a clash. The flowing figure looks beautiful from any direction and appears to change its form as the point of view moves. The enclosed lawn makes a good-sized area for children's play, though it – and the hedge – will need regular cutting to preserve the precise shape.

3 An ornamental seat, shaded by a canopy overgrown with climbing roses, is set against a side wall in a second seating area. (Because the lawn takes up so much space it is preferable to have two small seating areas instead of one larger.) On each side are matching antique terracotta lions on plinths, standing sentinel. To preserve the symmetry of the garden, the seat is balanced on the cross axis by a stone pyramid on a plinth set in the border opposite. This becomes the main focal point from the seat, and a gap in the low box hedge permits an uninterrupted view.

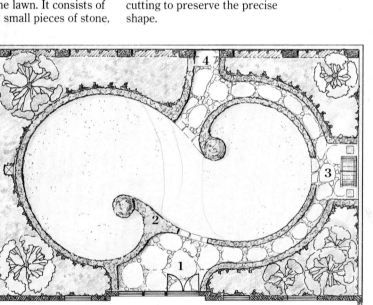

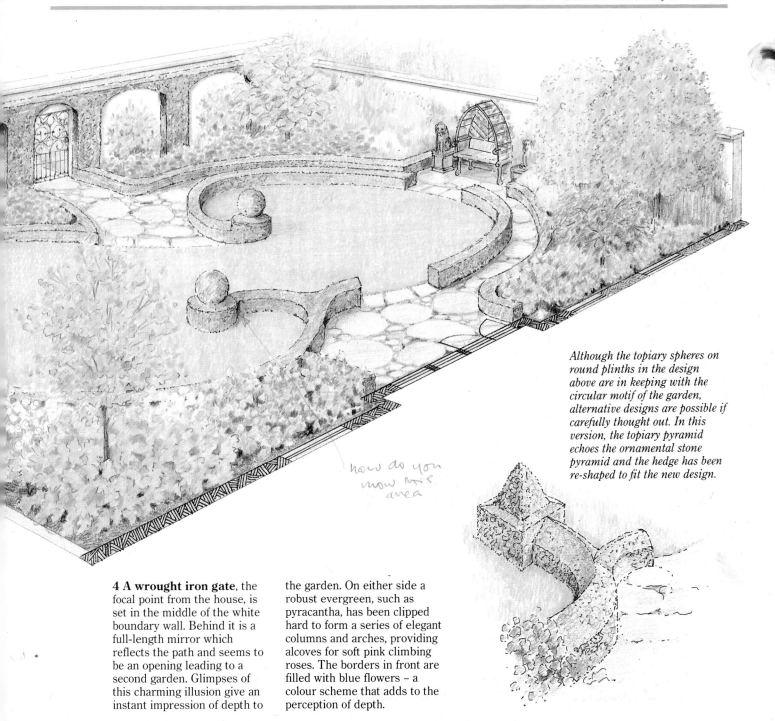

how do you mow this area

Although the topiary spheres on round plinths in the design above are in keeping with the circular motif of the garden, alternative designs are possible if carefully thought out. In this version, the topiary pyramid echoes the ornamental stone pyramid and the hedge has been re-shaped to fit the new design.

4 A wrought iron gate, the focal point from the house, is set in the middle of the white boundary wall. Behind it is a full-length mirror which reflects the path and seems to be an opening leading to a second garden. Glimpses of this charming illusion give an instant impression of depth to the garden. On either side a robust evergreen, such as pyracantha, has been clipped hard to form a series of elegant columns and arches, providing alcoves for soft pink climbing roses. The borders in front are filled with blue flowers – a colour scheme that adds to the perception of depth.

Left *A formal clipped box motif centred on a silvery metallic sphere offers a strong, static focal point, continually drawing the eye back to the pattern of a circle within a square. Flanked by equally neat, ground-hugging planting, the low formal layout anchors the freer shapes of soaring perennials beyond. Such a strong internal structure works well as a counterweight to distract from an awkwardly shaped plot.*

Right *With its foliage contrasts between swordlike and grassy spikes and larger shapely leaves, planting round an informal pool draws the eye downwards, away from garden boundaries. As in the plan for an informal garden (opposite above), the simple timber bridge suits the informal style of the garden and allows the planting and water to claim full attention.*

A formal garden

This highly formal design gives the garden a strong internal structure. The reflecting water in the pool and the pale-coloured paving surrounding it makes the centre very light, and adds depth to the garden. Further depth is suggested by the semicircular arbour set against the back wall – which gives the impression of extending further back – and the placing of four matched small trees towards but not at the corners, so that the space behind the trees makes the garden seem more extensive.

The design is highly symmetrical and there are two strong axes, with the shorter emphasized by the path either side of the circular pool. Opposite the arbour, which shelters a decorative seat, is the main seating area next to the house – again paved with light coloured stone, on which are two planters. At each side of the garden a pair of figures act as focal points to the cross axis.

The symmetry is reinforced by the four matching trees and by the four flower beds surrounding the central circular area, which are filled with just one plant type – for example box or lavender. The surrounding area is grassed, making a good space for children's play, but could easily be covered in gravel, for ease of maintenance, or ivy, without spoiling the design.

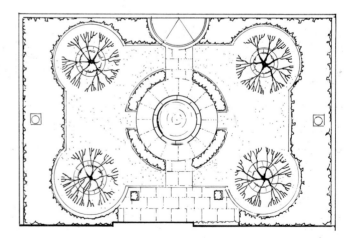

An informal garden

The curving organic lines used in this design both disguise the wide shallow shape and, by hiding some parts from view, suggest extra distance. Next to the house a semi-circular paved area on which tables and chairs are placed makes a spacious terrace, with a wide vista. Directly opposite across the lawn is a small clump of trees, with the far border gently curving back either side, a planting arrangement that draws attention away from the line of the boundary.

On one side is a raised circular lawn in an open sunny position, with a curved bench seat under a sheltering tree. From here and from the terrace the main focus is a small pond partly screened by its surrounding planting of tall water and bog plants. Grass paths wind round either side to its narrowest point where a small timber bridge crosses it. Tucked away in one corner is a garden shed, completely screened from the main area by trees and other planting.

THE FRONT GARDEN

Front gardens typically tend to be shallow compared to their width and care must be taken that the design is not over-whelmed by the space necessary to accommodate a car. Here, the shape of the drive-way, while providing good space for turning, is perfectly balanced by the shapes used in the layout of the whole garden.

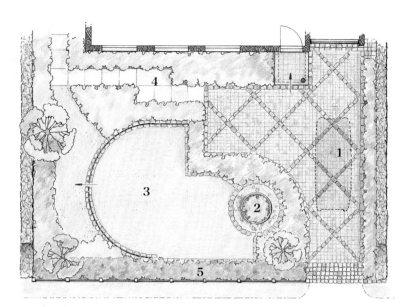

1 The drive is paved with strong square bricks or tiles, with setts in a contrasting colour laid in a diamond pattern. Its shape is largely determined by the position of the garage, the need for direct access to it and the provision of space for turning and parking. The 'shadow' car on the plan is typical in size of a medium-to-large family car and shows how much space is needed.

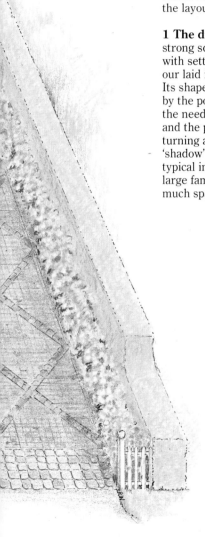

2 A large terracotta bowl filled with flowers is the visual focus of the whole garden. It is surrounded by pebbles, which make a good foil, and then on one side by a border that curves gracefully around it. The border is filled with massed planting of one shrub or flower that matches the planting lining the other side of the drive.

3 The central lawn is on two levels, adding further interest to the site. The shape of the lower level complements the shape of the curved bed by the drive and is marked out by setts, which provide a harmonious continuity in use of materials and a practical mowing edge.

4 A paved path, in a colour that matches the setts, leads round the front of the house to a gateway at the side. Beds next to the front of a house are often, as here, shady and so blue flowers, which look good in shade, have been planted, with brighter ones added where the bed juts out to meet the porch.

5 The front boundary is marked by a white-painted picket fence in front of a rose hedge, making a delightful picture from the road. An evergreen hedge marks the boundary on each side, its height reduced near the road to give a clear view on leaving.

Drives and car-parking areas need not have uninteresting surfaces; they can contribute to the attractiveness of the garden and play an important role if the surface takes up a large proportion of the space. Shown here is an alternative to the design used in the illustrated garden: chamfered bricks make the diamond-pattern framework and are infilled with coloured concrete setts laid in a curved pattern.

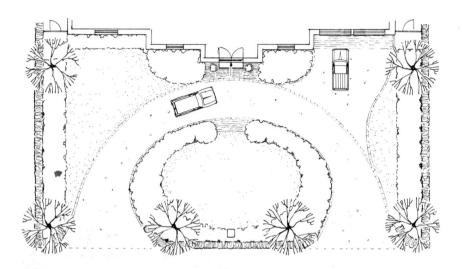

A large garden

Where space allows, it is safer and more convenient to have a drive with two entrances – an 'in and out' drive. Here the openings are wide, allowing easy turning to or from either direction when entering or exiting.

The overall design of the garden is formal but softened by the gentle curves of the drive. An edging of bricks prevents the lateral spread of the gravel surface, and the bricks continue the semicircular pattern across the spur that leads to the garage, in order to preserve symmetry. Areas of grass each side, edged with formal borders backed by hedges, balance the design, and six matching trees emphasize the symmetry.

The height of the front hedge can depend on how important it is to hide the road but in any case, from the house, this design focuses attention on the central area. Steps from the drive lead up to a soft oval of grass enclosed by a curving border. A gap in the border by the steps permits an uninterrupted view from the front door to a focal point – a statue or other decorative figure – on the far side.

Above *This driveway has a tweedy, woven texture that makes a good functional surface, but plays several design roles, too. The patterning of setts enables paths converging from different angles to flow together in interesting cross-currents while maintaining the strong circular motif. Flecks of contrasting material provide a good way of marrying in a nearby feature (such as a brick wall) to make it harmonize.*

Right *The formality of the circular path in this front garden is not reinforced by an equally formal approach to planting. Instead, a relaxed mass of perennials fills the beds and softens the design.*

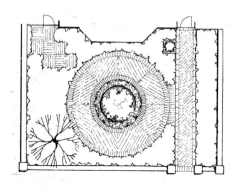

A small garden

This tiny plot is typical of many found fronting town houses or cottages. Here there is no question of car parking.

A simple formal design fits this space best. A brick path leads directly to the front door, and a brick circle surrounds the garden's centrepiece – a large bowl filled with bright seasonal bedding and under planted with ivy or other evergreen ground cover. To one side, by the house a criss-cross brick path leads to a side entrance; to the other, pots filled with more seasonal plants brighten the entrance.

Grass would not be suitable for such a confined space, so easy-care perennial planting fills the unpaved areas. An ornamental tree, such as a small magnolia or Japanese maple, decorates one corner and a low brick wall surrounds the garden.

L-SHAPED GARDENS

An L-shaped site comes ready-made with assets that people with a plain slab of garden have to create for themselves. The two arms of an L will immediately comprise two compartments partly separated from each other, and you may be able to subdivide them into more.

In an ideal plot the two sections of the L will be well proportioned and offer all the benefits of a pair of small rectangular or square gardens. For example, you can have formality in one 'garden' and a natural-looking layout in another. If there is a part that is tucked away out of sight, it can accommodate the activities you don't want right under your nose – functional vegetable-growing or noisy ball games for example – or you can exploit its potential for mystery. Screened off, a hidden compartment can conceal a private restful haven. Alternatively, you can plan a wilderness beyond the more formally laid out garden near the house, to provide a refuge for wildlife, as in the gardens on pages 118–121.

If you design the link with the main garden carefully, visitors will come upon the hidden area as a pleasant surprise – an extra bonus to the garden tour – perhaps entered through a secret archway in what appeared to be a boundary, or explored along an enticing path that curves away past a screen of shrubs. In the woodland garden on page 119 the entrance to the secluded wooded area is via a narrow timber bridge that crosses an L-shaped pond.

When the two angles of the L are not subdivided in such a way but are more open, you will need to create a cohesive ground plan that holds the different sections of the garden together. The rhythm of any geometric shapes and patterns used must somehow cope with the perhaps uncomfortably different proportions of an irregular L. The plan for a double garden on page 116 exploits the shape perfectly by positioning a circular lawn in the angle of the L, with a specimen tree as its linch pin. In the wildlife garden on pages 118–19 the 'hinge' between the two parts of the plot consists of an irregularly shaped pond. Both solutions work well as pivots serving both as focal points from the two ends of the garden and providing an absorbing source of interest in their own right.

The position of the house in relation to an L-shape is crucial: sometimes it will form the inside corner and be flanked by garden on two sides; sometimes the house will open on to one 'arm' or end of the L, and the garden will turn away out of sight. Each plot has unique facets of aspect and so on, which you can make the most of by clever planning. One arm of a small garden may well be predominantly shady, for example; the classic ingredients of paving and ivy turn this into a tranquil green garden room, or less formal planting makes a tree-lined walk, as in the family garden on page 116.

Roof gardens

The roof gardens on pages 122–123 illustrate the very special case of an L-shaped garden operating under a particular set of restraints, with the exposure of the site and the need for lightweight materials paramount. However, you could adapt the main design solution to any L-shaped site on a small scale – the attractive pergola, in particular, can be used anywhere to create an intimate and secluded atmosphere.

In this generously proportioned L-shaped garden the compositional elements take the form of full-sized trees and extensive tracts of lawn. In early autumn the brilliant foliage of the amelanchier at the inner corner of the pivot of the two arms of the L contrasts with the green backdrop of handsome evergreen and deciduous trees, including yew, cedar and Prunus × subhirtella 'Autumnalis'. The table and chairs positioned for enjoying the view down both arms of the L are made of robust timber, in keeping with the serene woodland atmosphere of the surroundings. Nearby a bronze 'sun king' sculpture adds a subtle note of ornament, acting rather like some guardian spirit of the place.

THE FORMAL GARDEN

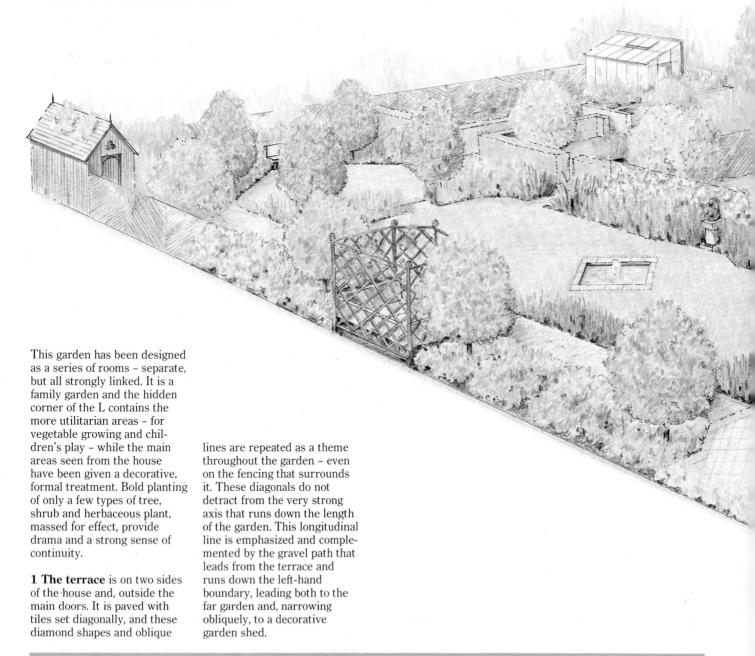

This garden has been designed as a series of rooms – separate, but all strongly linked. It is a family garden and the hidden corner of the L contains the more utilitarian areas – for vegetable growing and children's play – while the main areas seen from the house have been given a decorative, formal treatment. Bold planting of only a few types of tree, shrub and herbaceous plant, massed for effect, provide drama and a strong sense of continuity.

1 The terrace is on two sides of the house and, outside the main doors. It is paved with tiles set diagonally, and these diamond shapes and oblique lines are repeated as a theme throughout the garden – even on the fencing that surrounds it. These diagonals do not detract from the very strong axis that runs down the length of the garden. This longitudinal line is emphasized and complemented by the gravel path that leads from the terrace and runs down the left-hand boundary, leading both to the far garden and, narrowing obliquely, to a decorative garden shed.

2 The diamond-shaped pool
with a fountain is the central
focus of the garden 'room'
nearest the house, but also
provides a focal point from the
far end. On one side is a pretty
trellis pavilion, covered in
honeysuckle or another sweet-
scented climber. Balancing this
cross axis is a sculpture on a
plinth set against the border on
the other side. At the far end
of the rectangular lawn the
borders narrow, forming a
gateway at the brick-paved
threshold to the far garden.

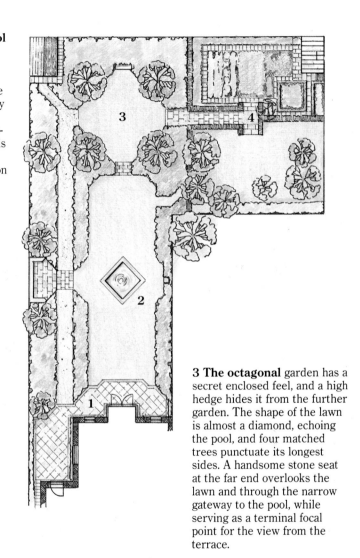

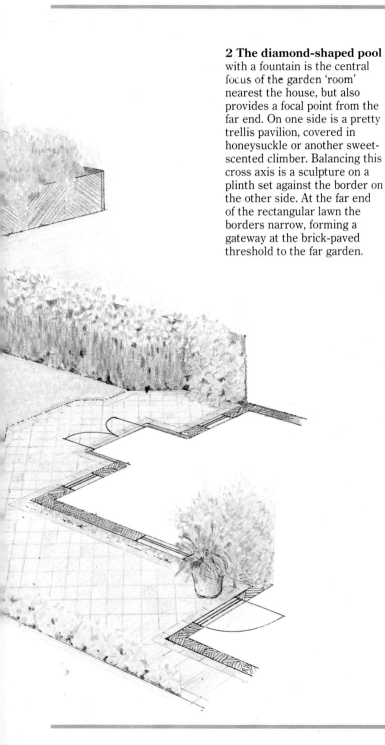

3 The octagonal garden has a
secret enclosed feel, and a high
hedge hides it from the further
garden. The shape of the lawn
is almost a diamond, echoing
the pool, and four matched
trees punctuate its longest
sides. A handsome stone seat
at the far end overlooks the
lawn and through the narrow
gateway to the pool, while
serving as a terminal focal
point for the view from the
terrace.

4 A brick-paved path leads
from the octagonal garden to
the two more functional gardens, which are separated from
each other by high hedges. On
one side is a vegetable garden
and greenhouse and on the
other a simple expanse of lawn
for play equipment and games,
dotted with a few trees.

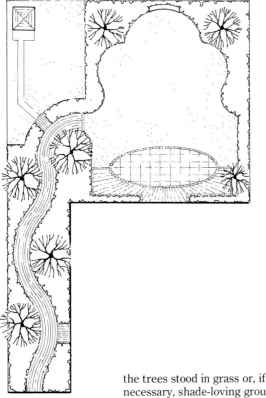

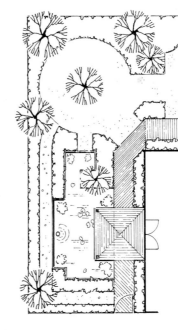

A family garden

The L shape of this garden is again formed by following the house walls but one side is very narrow. This type of plot is often found with terraced or semi-detached houses. Here the narrowness of the one side has almost been made a feature by giving it a dramatic and intriguing serpentine path that winds round small trees (positioned to give the path reason to curve). The brick path is surrounded by colourful herbaceous planting, but this area would be equally effective if the trees stood in grass or, if necessary, shade-loving ground cover.

The path winds to the main garden – a wide formal area of terrace and lawn, strictly symmetrical yet continuing the theme of soft curves. Next to the house an elaborately shaped and detailed paved terrace looks out across the broad lawn whose scalloped shape gently narrows to a decorative curved seat.

Completing the whole garden is a separate area in the far corner, here devoted to children's activities, with a lawn and playhouse. This could, be a vegetable plot.

A double garden

In this garden the L is formed because the plot follows the house walls, and it has been designed to present two quite different gardens for each arm of the L. The success of this approach depends on the area that both separates and links the two. Here, a circular lawn with a specimen tree at its centre copes beautifully with the change of direction, being visually satisfying in its own right and fitting perfectly with each garden. The specimen tree makes an impressive feature seen from either arm, and becomes the pivot or linch pin of the whole design.

On one side of the house is a water garden. Patio doors open on to a raised timber deck for sitting and sunbathing, which projects over a tranquil formal pond. On one side, a decking path leads from it to a gate, on the other turning the house corner. A gravel path goes from the decking path round the pond and down to the circular lawn.

The garden on the other side of the house consists of an open, spacious formal lawn. Doors open on a decking terrace that looks across the lawn to a focal point, such as a birdbath, against the far border. On one side the lawn narrows and leads to the circular garden. On the other side a bench seat provides a place from which to appreciate the specimen tree.

Whether formally designed or, as here, planned to resemble a natural pond, a pool that runs right up to a terrace of decking surrounding the house adds an extra dimension to a garden. Even with a long thin shape the pool will fill the space and make it seem larger. This is a dramatic way of treating one arm of an L shape, as in the double garden plan above.

THE WILDLIFE GARDEN

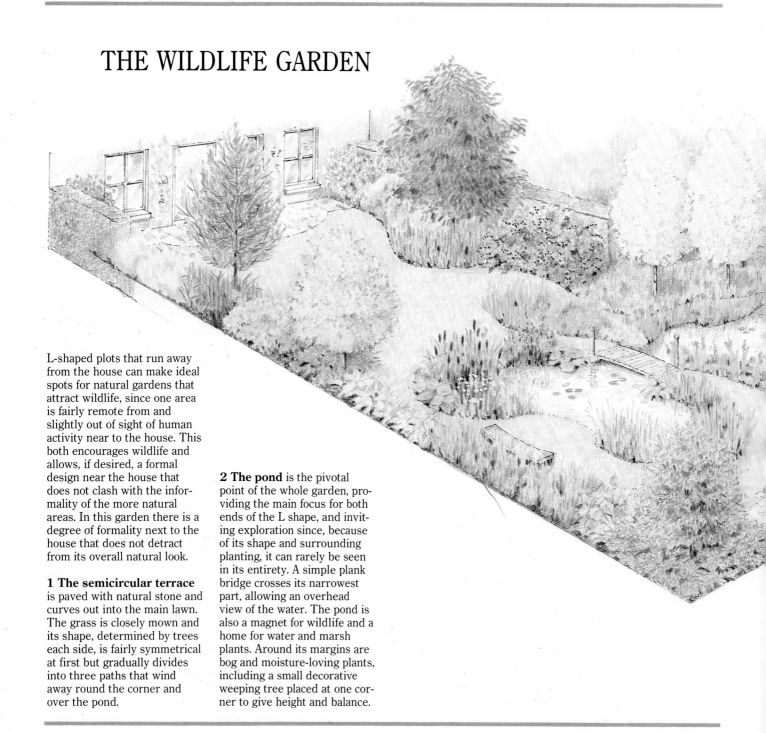

L-shaped plots that run away from the house can make ideal spots for natural gardens that attract wildlife, since one area is fairly remote from and slightly out of sight of human activity near to the house. This both encourages wildlife and allows, if desired, a formal design near the house that does not clash with the informality of the more natural areas. In this garden there is a degree of formality next to the house that does not detract from its overall natural look.

1 The semicircular terrace is paved with natural stone and curves out into the main lawn. The grass is closely mown and its shape, determined by trees each side, is fairly symmetrical at first but gradually divides into three paths that wind away round the corner and over the pond.

2 The pond is the pivotal point of the whole garden, providing the main focus for both ends of the L shape, and inviting exploration since, because of its shape and surrounding planting, it can rarely be seen in its entirety. A simple plank bridge crosses its narrowest part, allowing an overhead view of the water. The pond is also a magnet for wildlife and a home for water and marsh plants. Around its margins are bog and moisture-loving plants, including a small decorative weeping tree placed at one corner to give height and balance.

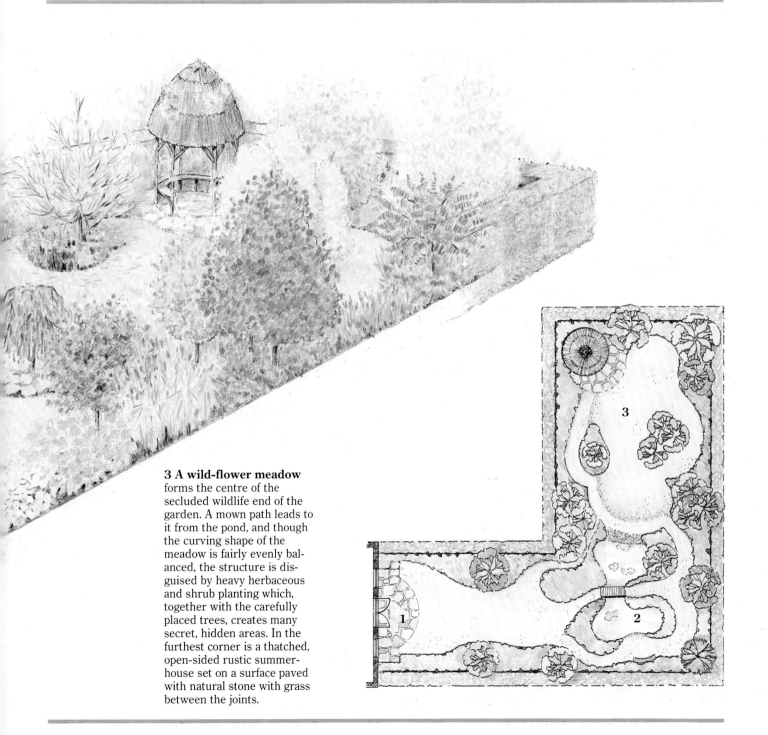

3 A wild-flower meadow
forms the centre of the
secluded wildlife end of the
garden. A mown path leads to
it from the pond, and though
the curving shape of the
meadow is fairly evenly balanced, the structure is disguised by heavy herbaceous
and shrub planting which,
together with the carefully
placed trees, creates many
secret, hidden areas. In the
furthest corner is a thatched,
open-sided rustic summer-
house set on a surface paved
with natural stone with grass
between the joints.

Left *The simple lines of an arching bridge make a slightly more sophisticated alternative to the simple plank bridge suggested for the wildlife garden on the previous pages and for the woodland garden (above right). Although this is a more selfconscious 'design', and its arching shape will be more obvious as it rises from ground level, the natural materials and gentle curves suit the informal setting well.*

Above *As in the woodland garden plan on this page, angular, formal elements can be successfully juxtaposed with an area of natural planting leading to woodland. The foliage plants have been carefully grouped together but are allowed to grow freely, and the sharp triangular geometry of the table and stools is reflected in the paving, but softened, as grass and small plants are allowed to encroach on the tiles.*

A woodland garden

In this design there is a sharp distinction between the formal and informal styles used in the garden, with angular, formal features jutting right into the wild area. However, since this is an area of natural woodland, the division between the two is quickly hidden by the thickly planted trees.

The arm of the L next to the house is asymmetrically formal. A paved terrace is set at an angle, giving a diagonal view of the garden. This use of diagonal lines is continued, with an angular lawn creating interesting border shapes and partly hidden areas. A seat sheltered by a tree is both the prize for venturing to the far corner of

the lawn and a perfect position from which to view the pond and the woodland.

A bark path leads from the terrace along one side of the formal garden and turns the corner towards the woodland. Here it becomes a simple timber bridge, and crosses an L-shaped pond. The pond is designed to echo the shape of the lawn and, more subtly, the garden as a whole.

The thickly wooded area is secluded and inviting – a haven for wildlife and promising adventure. It has been left as natural as possible, the only provision for visitors being the winding bark path and a bench seat in the corner of a small clearing.

THE ROOF GARDEN

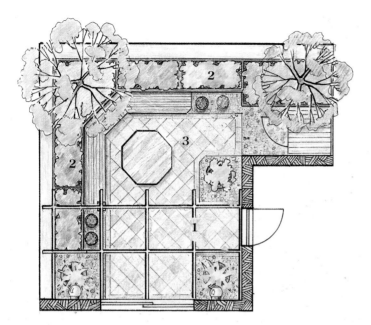

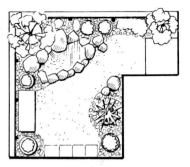

Roof gardens are frequently L shaped, since a stairway or some other access point usually intrudes into the open expanse of roof.

There are a number of constraints on the design of roof gardens. Obviously, the roof's water proofing must not be interfered with, and its structure needs to be strong enough to support the extra weight. As in this design the main planting – and any other heavy weight – is best supported around the perimeter close to the structural walls.

The plants need to be hardy enough to survive being grown in containers, in which the effects of heat and cold tend to be more extreme. They also need to withstand the stronger winds often found at roof level. More tender plants and annuals can be used to provide changing seasonal colour.

Some kind of shelter, screen or filtering windbreak is needed, and it is worth noting that in historic or conservation areas there may be regulations limiting or prohibiting screens or plants being visible from street level.

1 The pergola is a vital part of this design. Not only does it provide welcome shade and a support for flowering climbers, but also makes the whole space more intimate by reducing the view which, in many roof gardens, is too wide and open. It is fixed to the walls, seat and planter for stability.

2 The main planting is situated round the edge, against the parapet walls, and is contained in portable timber planters of varying heights, filled with lightweight, moisture-retentive compost. Two small

trees punctuate the corners, adding height and balancing the design. One is growing over and helping to camouflage a water tank or cooling system unit situated round the corner. Most rooftops have some unattractive feature such as this, which might also be hidden by trellis or plants in pots.

3 The central area is paved with slate laid with waterproof adhesive; any lightweight thin-section durable paving would make an appropriate alternative. In one corner and extending along two sides is a timber seat, partly sheltered by a tree. It has a hinged top for storage – roof gardens are normally small and so space-saving is important – and surrounds a matching timber table. Around the rest of the paving, areas of lightweight gravel make a good foil for smaller containers.

A simple garden
This is a plainer, and somewhat cheaper, alternative. The garden is surrounded by trellis which, being mainly unadorned by climbing plants, gives a sensation of intimacy without completely blocking the wide view.

The main focus of the garden is a small, very shallow pool, with a trickling fountain and a black lining that gives an attractive mirror effect. It is surrounded by high-quality artificial rocks made of glass-reinforced plastic or concrete; these look convincingly like stone but weigh only a fraction of the real thing.

The central area is laid with lightweight gravel – an excellent surface for roof gardens – with a few thin-section paving slabs at the door threshold. To one side is a simple bench seat. The two trees remain to give height and balance, but there are fewer plants. Some are in decorative pots, others have their planters hidden by the surrounding stones and gravel.

GARDENS SURROUNDING THE HOUSE

More than any other layout, every garden surrounding a house is an individual case. Many variables combine to make each situation unique: the total garden area and whether its boundary is regular or irregular; the shape and size of the house and its garages and outbuildings, and how the buildings are arranged on the site; the direction and type of access, and the general lie of the land.

However, you can find common factors in planning for these large gardens. Because the approach to the house is made through part of the garden, and more garden forms the background, you have a good opportunity to provide the kind of setting that displays the house to best advantage. The examples on pages 126–7 and on pages 130–31 both create an imposing area in front of the house with a curving driveway focused on a circular centrepiece. The first of these examples is approached along a short stretch of tree-lined drive, and another such avenue provides the entrance to the formal garden shown on page 129. Even on a smaller scale, you can use an avenue to contribute a touch of grandeur.

With a relatively large amount of space available, you can easily set aside special-purpose areas within the garden. Private, secluded areas can offer a choice of sun or shade at a given time, and you can situate them near the house or somewhere tucked away in the secret depths of the garden.

Functional areas for parking, kitchen gardens or sports activities need not intrude on the ornamental or pleasure garden. Indeed, if you screen these different zones with trees, shrubs, hedges and attractive fencing you create opportunities for massed planting that can be beautiful in their own right. You can also use the routes and paths that link the different areas to provide the structural backbone of the garden. Well-proportioned, and winding in curves out of sight, they will unify the various elements and entice the visitor to explore the garden.

A variation on the path theme that is ideal for a large garden is a generously proportioned pergola. You can use this structure to break up an area into smaller sections or compartments, and it will also provide a sense of containment and intimacy for those walking beneath which is often missed in an extensive plot, however beautifully laid out. The long rose walk in the grassy garden shown on page 132 occupies a narrow strip towards one boundary, but you could also place an allee in a more central position to good effect. Arbours, summer houses and gazebos – such as in the garden on page 130 – provide intimate areas, and resting places that are all the more necessary when the garden tour is a lengthy one.

A garden surrounding the house usually offers scope for a combination of formality and informality; this is especially illustrated in the garden on pages 126–7, which contains symmetrical lawns and borders, offering classically formal vistas, with a wildflower meadow and natural woodland. You can lose a rectangular boundary in dense naturalistic planting or exploit it for its structural guidelines. In an irregularly shaped site, geometric elements can be created in areas of their own – the family garden on pages 130–31 uses a theme of circles – or can take their cue from the straight lines of the house. Some kind of more or less formal area such as a terrace is always a good idea next to the house, and is included in all the designs that follow.

As you explore a well-designed garden that surrounds the house, you find a succession of garden pictures, partly hidden from each other, and so gaining interest, with carefully placed features that draw the visitor onwards. On this side of the house the lawn and border meet in relaxed curves that lose the straight boundary beyond and a large tree placed as a lawn specimen balances the mass of the house. In the foreground a path promises a quick route to see what lies just around the corner. In the distance a seat set at an angle implies that the view from the vantage point is well worth studying at leisure.

THE SPORTS GARDEN

Large gardens provide good opportunities for designs for families who enjoy sports, such as swimming and tennis. Pools and, especially, tennis courts are often not attractive to look at, particularly in winter, and so are best sited away or hidden from the house. This garden is divided into several different areas, formal and informal, and easily accommodates both a swimming pool and tennis court as well as grassy areas for ball games and children's play, and even a few secluded spaces for private relaxation. Many paths link each area, inviting exploration.

1 A large weeping tree, directly in line with the main entrance to the house, forms the centrepiece to the spacious drive. The curved end of the formal front lawn – formed by an evergreen hedge – echoes the curve of the drive. The hedge, while acting as a foil for a small statue placed as a focal point, is balanced by an evergreen hedge on the other side of the drive, which screens the vegetable garden. The whole of the front area serves as an open spacious setting for the house and is shielded from the road by a row of trees.

2 Stone paving surrounds the house, forming a wide terrace at the back which leads out from a large conservatory. At the side is a small secluded garden, entirely formal, with a sunken pond and a stone seat. There is quite a contrast between this intimate area and the main garden at the back,

although both are formal. The broad steps leading from the large terrace increase the sense of space created by the curved expanse of lawn. The view from the terrace continues along the main axis to a large tree at the end of the tree-lined rectangular lawn. On the cross axis a focal point, hidden from the terrace, faces an exit from this formal part of the garden.

3 The swimming pool is approached by paths from various directions and is surrounded by fairly tall planting, shielding it from winds and screening it from the house. The pool's shape is informal, fitting the overall style of this part of the garden. At one end a small summerhouse with doors on two sides doubles as a chang-

ing room. On one side it looks towards the pool; on the other it overlooks a natural meadow garden. This area is large, but the placement of trees and the curving shape of the meadow lawn ensure that many parts are hidden from view.

4 The tennis court is at the furthest part of the garden, shielded by tall planting, and surrounded by dark green wire mesh that blends into the background. At one end is a small pavilion, for rest and refreshment, and paths behind it lead to a densely wooded area. Hidden in the centre is a secluded dell, an open but private clearing with a small seat for quiet contemplation.

The view from the main terrace of the garden on the previous page looks longer because the curving borders restrict the view of the far lawn, so further increasing the sense of distance. Brick paving continues the oval shape of the rear lawn. The matched planting of trees draws the eye along the vista to a large tree planted as a lawn specimen, with a wooden seat surrounding its base, and set against the backdrop of a curving evergreen hedge.

Although in hot climates a swimming pool can be a dramatic and integral part of a stylish garden design, there are often good reasons for surrounding a swimming pool with a screen of planting. Bathers appreciate the shelter – from wind and/or sun – and the privacy. Furthermore, a pool is essentially functional and artificial, even when it is designed in a supposedly 'natural' shape, and may not blend in with the other components that make up the garden, especially in an informal, natural setting. And, of course, a swimming pool can seem very forlorn seen on a cold winter's day. In a separate garden compartment, as here, the swimming pool plays a part in a pleasing composition of its own. Surrounding stonework and plant containers harmonize, and a bank of plants pouring over the boundaries and creeping down to the water's edge help integrate the pool with the garden beyond.

An informal garden

This garden narrows towards the far end, and so the tennis court has been fitted in obliquely, following one line of the boundary. Trees and shrubs provide a screen, and this would also be a good position for a swimming pool. At one end a large semicircular paved seating area contains a bench seat and a barbecue and space for *al fresco* parties.

Between the tennis court and the house, carefully planted trees and flowing borders disguise the straight sides of the plot and create a number of informal spaces. A seat tucked into the side border looks back towards the house and its wide paved terrace.

At the front, the drive is positioned to one side in order to leave as large a space as possible for a lawn used for play, especially ball games. The drive winds past trees, deliberately placed to determine its shape in a natural way, to a paved courtyard enclosed on two sides by the house and garages.

A formal garden

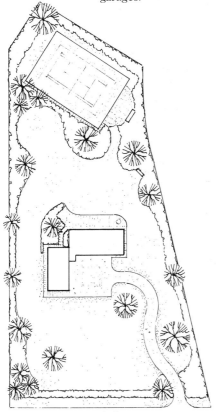

An informal garden

A formal garden

In this garden, again, as large an area as possible is wanted as a lawn for games, and here it has been placed behind the house, so that the drive does not take up any of its space.

The rear garden is symmetrically formal; the focal point at the far end is set in a semicircular bay echoing the shape of the terrace next to the house, and matching the two semicircular lawn bays on the cross axis. In one there is a seat, in the other an opening to a hidden path that runs along the side. Four matched trees are placed towards the corners, emphasizing the balance and the formality of the area.

The front garden's layout is asymmetrical. Since the small swimming pool is placed here, it needs some privacy. This shelter is provided by a tall evergreen hedge that turns at right angles from the front, becoming circular as it encloses the pool. A hexagonal summerhouse-cum-changing room is set in the corner overlooking the circular pool. A path winds from the opposite corner, round the hedge and through shrubbery and trees to a small paved terrace at the side of the house.

From the road, a small section of evergreen hedge is placed on the left-hand side for balance and the drive is lined with matching trees, making an impressive entrance.

THE FAMILY GARDEN

In gardens that surround the house, design strategies are often determined by the position of the house relative to the plot – for example it may be much nearer one boundary – or, if it is unusual, by the shape of the plot itself. This garden is a very irregular shape and this, together with the position of the house, creates some strangely proportioned areas. Nevertheless, a harmonious design has been made by the use of circles, curves and swirling shapes that create movement and continuity throughout the garden and invite exploration.

1 A tree-lined drive marks the entrance of the garden. It turns into a circle, with a tree and flower bed at its centre, leading to the front door of the house and, via a turning to the side, a garage and service area surrounded by trees and flower beds. A little secluded lawn with a sheltered seat is tucked away between the garage and the drive. The broad grass verges on all sides of the drive give a sense of space to the front garden.

2 The house is surrounded by a terrace on three sides, providing seating in sun or shade all day. Extra shade is provided on one side by a timber pergola; next to it runs a broad grass walk, gently winding round to the front. On the opposite side, a paved patio curves out into a circular lawn surrounded by trees and flower beds, where a stone seat beneath a tree provides a focal point and a narrow grass path winds out of sight.

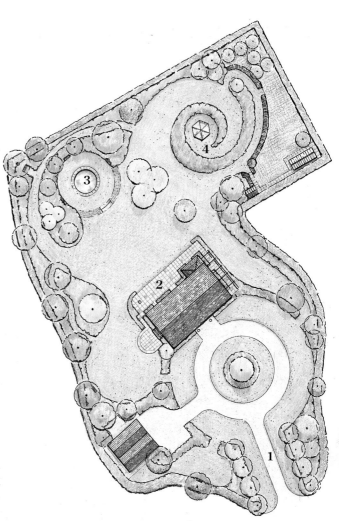

3 A circular reflecting pond at the centre of a slightly mysterious sunken area of grass lies on a direct axis from the main terrace at the rear of the house. Between is a large open lawn dotted with specimen trees. Three simple bench seats look inward towards the pond. Surrounding them, and acting as a foil to the pond, is a planting of trees and shrubs. Behind this is a curved and narrowing grass walk with a private seat tucked in a corner, almost hidden by trees and shrubs.

4 A 'swirling' lawn, with a pretty gazebo at its centre, provides the garden's most dramatic feature, and continues its curving theme. It is created by a spiral planting of a flowering hedge – such as a shrub or dog rose – and is edged on one side by a curving evergreen hedge that disguises the rectangular corners of the end of the plot. Behind this evergreen screen is a vegetable garden, workshop and greenhouse, and a small orchard.

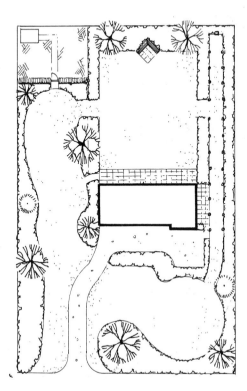

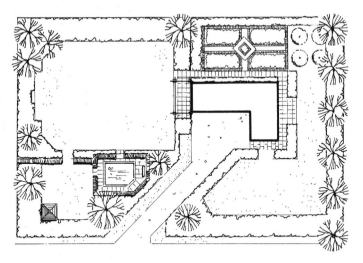

A grassy garden

In this plot, the house is very near the side boundary, so the narrowness of this area is extended and taken advantage of by making a long rose walk. This allée consists of a grass path lined with rope-linked poles, over which rambling roses are grown. It leads from the front garden to the very back, where a statue serves as its terminal focal point.

The rest of the garden consists of three large lawns that provide plenty of space for family games; tucked away in one corner is an enclosed vegetable garden. A long curving lawn with the vegetable plot at the end balances the allee on the other side. Behind the house is a spacious formal garden with a broad paved terrace and a rectangular lawn surrounded by formal borders. A diamond-shaped paved seating area with seats on two sides flanked by matching trees makes an elegant view from the house.

At the front, a boldly curving lawn and drive make an open setting for the house. Carefully placed trees and beds determine the shape of the lawn and allow the drive to widen along the front of the house, providing ample space for cars.

A formal garden

In this garden the L-shaped house is set rather near the back and side of the plot. This means more care is needed to provide secluded spaces – since they will not be shielded by the house. Here a series of large and small private, formal areas has been created, making a garden full of interest.

The drive approaches the house obliquely – a bold design feature that creates interesting shapes at the front. To the right-hand side, an enclosed, roughly L-shaped lawn echoes the shape of the house – which itself is almost completely surrounded by a paved terrace. A flowering hedge at the front, together with a formal line of trees at the side, creates privacy. Behind the house, taking advantage of the small space, is a pretty parterre.

The largest garden is at the left-hand side, and consists of an open rectangular lawn, framed by flower borders, with a stone seat as a focal point. From the terrace the view is framed by a pergola, which supports a flowering climber such as wisteria. Openings off the main lawn lead to two charming garden 'rooms', separate and secluded, yet linked. One is a small square of lawn, with a summerhouse in one corner, almost totally enclosed by trees and a tall flowering hedge on two sides and an evergreen hedge on the other. The other intimate 'room' contains a small pool with seats on a paved surround, and is completely enclosed by the evergreen hedge.

MAKING THE PLAN

There are four stages involved in making a plan for your garden: the site plan is an accurate record of the boundary and of all the main elements within it; analysis adds such details as changes in level, orientation and the quality of the soil; a functional plan indicates the position of the garden's intended main components; and, finally, the outline plan shows in detail the positions and shapes of each element in the garden.

The finishing touches to the outline plan include: choosing and specifying the materials for walls, fences and paving; the details of 'soft' landscaping, including lawns and plants; and the decorative and functional extras such as statues, furniture and lighting.

SURVEYING THE GARDEN

Measuring the plot takes a lot of time, so first find out if there is an existing plan with the deeds, or with the architect if the house has been built fairly recently. Check that it has been drawn accurately and to scale by taking some measurements and comparing the results with the plan. If no survey exists, or it is inadequate, the garden will have to be measured and drawn up.

Making your own plan is by far the best way to proceed as you will have to look at every corner of the garden, studying every feature and taking measurements. You will end up with valuable knowledge of the lie of the land. Make notes of all the information you gather: the trees and shrubs you want to retain, drain covers that may affect the run of the path or the position of a raised bed. And if, for example, you notice that walls and fences indicate a change of level, make a note as this will be useful when you reach the stage of making an analysis of the site which will include all aspects – both inside and outside the garden – that may affect the design.

Measuring the garden is much easier if you have the help of an assistant. Equipment should include a 30m (100ft) tape for long measurements, a 3m (10ft) retractable steel tape for shorter ones and a scale rule (very useful as an instant reference but if preferred a normal rule will do).

To draw the plan, you will need a pencil, an eraser, a pair of compasses, a direction compass and a large sheet of graph paper. A clipboard or other portable hard surface on which to lay the paper is a great help as a mobile centre of operations.

The simplest ways to take measurements of the plot are 'sighting off' and 'triangulation'. Both provide a detailed breakdown of each available area in the garden. Sighting off is the technique to use if the house is set squarely in a regular-shaped plot. Triangulation is used to measure a plot of irregular shape and, in conjunction with sighting off, to measure a garden that includes angled or curved boundaries. Triangles are drawn to establish the exact position of points of reference such as corners of the boundary, trees and paths.

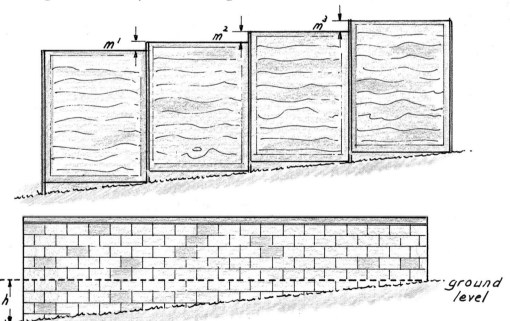

Walls and fences may indicate that the land is on a slope. Assuming that fence panels have been put in level (this can easily be checked with a spirit level), measure the rising steps formed by the panels and add them together to provide an estimate of the rise or fall over the length of the fence. Similarly, brick walls are normally built to a true level. By simply noting at the highest point where the join of a course of bricks starts at ground level and following the joint to the end of the wall, you can see how much the ground has fallen relative to that wall.

THE SITE PLAN

Start by pacing out the garden in at least two directions to give you an indication of the overall size. A pace is the equivalent of 1m (3ft). Work out, roughly, how the plan will fit on the graph paper. Now start taking exact measurements, beginning with the house: measure the outside wall lengths and draw them up. Note the position of windows and doors (and whether the doors open outwards or inwards) and which rooms are where. This will enable you to make the most of the views from each window and to consider such practicalities as positioning a patio outside the living room, or a vegetable garden within easy access of the kitchen.

Once the house walls have been plotted to scale, you are ready to use the sighting off and triangulation techniques to measure the adjacent land.

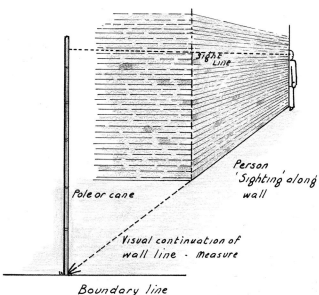

Sight Line

Person 'Sighting' along wall

Pole or cane

Visual continuation of wall line - measure

Boundary line

For sighting off stand behind one corner of the house at a point where the wall is seen as a fine line. Look beyond to the boundary and ask an assistant to mark with a pole or cane the point where the boundary and line of vision cross.

Continue this process around the garden using each wall as a sight line (right). Then measure from the house to each pole and the distances from pole to pole. Scale down your measurements and draw them on the plan.

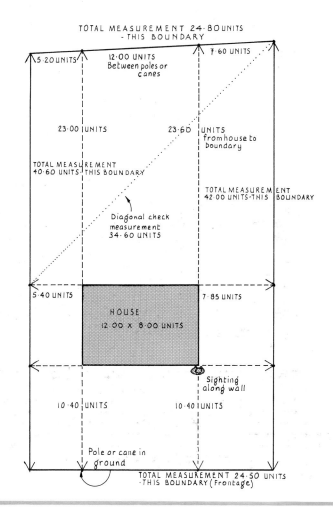

TOTAL MEASUREMENT 24·80 UNITS - THIS BOUNDARY

5·20 UNITS   12·00 UNITS Between poles or canes   7·60 UNITS

23·00 UNITS   23·60 UNITS from house to boundary

TOTAL MEASUREMENT 40·60 UNITS - THIS BOUNDARY

TOTAL MEASUREMENT 42·00 UNITS - THIS BOUNDARY

Diagonal check measurement 34·60 UNITS

5·40 UNITS   7·85 UNITS

HOUSE 12·00 X 8·00 UNITS

Sighting along wall

10·40 UNITS   10·40 UNITS

Pole or cane in ground

TOTAL MEASUREMENT 24·50 UNITS · THIS BOUNDARY (Frontage)

For triangulation use the house walls as base lines from which to plot the triangles. Take corner 1 facing house wall A–B. Measure the distance between A and 1, scale it down and convert into a 'radius' (the distance between pencil point and compasses point). Place the point of the compasses on house corner A and draw a broad arc in the approximate direction of corner 1. Repeat the exercise using the distance between corner 1 and house corner B. The point where the two arcs cross is the point of corner 1.

Repeat this process around the entire plot, checking accuracy with supplementary measurements: for example, once corner 2 has been measured against house wall A–B, it can be checked against corner 1 using the line B–2 as the base line of a new triangle.

If a boundary is curved between two points (for example, points 1 and 5), create a base line between the points and 'off-sets' – that is, points on the curved boundary – measured from the base line at 90 degrees to it and at regular distances. The way in which the boundary curves will determine the numbers of, and distances, between, the off-sets necessary for accurate plotting: a gentle curve requires fewer off-sets than an angular one.

Where there is an area which is impossible to measure over or through, for example an expanse of water or a group of dense shrubs, establish its outline by using off-sets. Construct base lines and work off-sets inwards from them.

In large gardens, the process of triangulation can be built up so that an entire garden is covered and measured accordingly. Using two tape measures, leave one on the ground as a base line, while you measure the off-sets and other distances with the other.

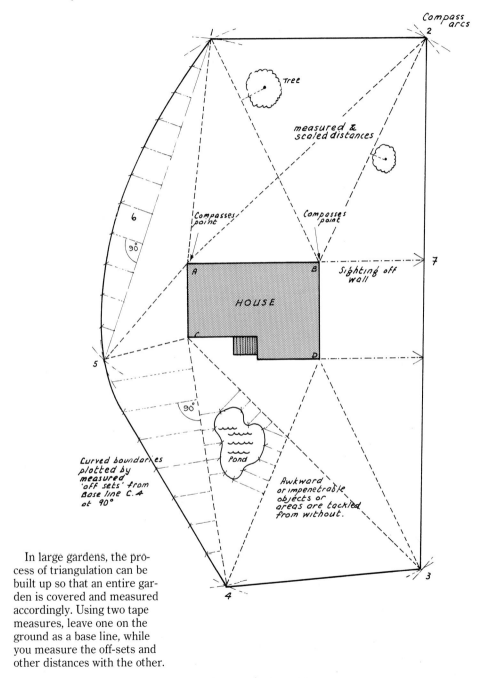

Compass arcs

Tree

measured & scaled distances

Compasses point

Compasses point

6

90°

Sighting off wall

A   B

HOUSE

C

D

5

90°

Pond

Curved boundaries plotted by measured 'off sets' from Base line C.4 at 90°

Awkward or impenetrable objects or areas are tackled from without.

7

1

2

3

4

ANALYSING THE PLOT

A typical site-analysis plan will include changes in level, orientation, noting good or bad views, and a soil analysis.

Changes in level are shown in boxes on the plan, starting at a chosen 'standard' measurement, or datum (marked as 0.00). They indicate where land rises (pluses relative to the datum) or falls (minuses, also relative to the datum). In gardens made up mostly of grass and plants it probably will not be necessary to record levels, especially if the slopes are gentle or nonexistent. If, however, flat areas are to be created on sloping ground, possibly requiring retaining walls, embankments and steps, then a record of the changes in level will be essential.

It can be difficult to work out accurately the rise and fall of the ground without special equipment and on difficult sites it may be worth getting a level survey done professionally. But if complete accuracy is not essential, look at existing features as indications of changes in level. Fences and walls both provide good guidance (see page 134).

Orientation or aspect is another vital piece of information. The direction a garden faces will have a profound effect upon its design, determining where the shadows fall, from which direction the prevailing winds will blow, and so on. This, in turn, will dictate the position of sitting areas,

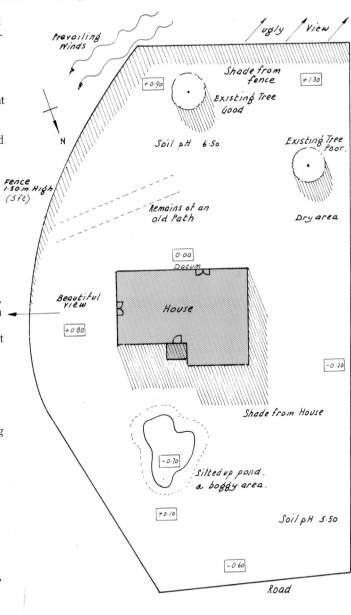

borders, vegetable gardens, swimming pools and many other features that call for a sheltered or sunny position. You should record the areas of shade, and remember that in winter the sun is lower in the sky and will therefore cast far more shade than in summer.

Elements outside the garden can affect what goes on within it. For example, a neighbour's high trees may cast shade or drop leaves in the garden. You should also note beautiful or ugly views so that you can appropriately take advantage of them or screen them.

Soil analysis, in terms of its pH value (degree of alkalinity or acidity), may vary slightly over a garden, especially a large one. Degrees of pH range from approximately 5 (acid) to 8 (alkaline), with 6.5 being neutral. Simple testing kits with explanatory leaflets are available from most garden centres. They are not expensive, and certainly less than the cost of several plants dying because the soil has the wrong pH for their needs.

Soil type and drainage also need to be analysed. Find out whether your soil type is clay, sand or loam. Damp areas may indicate that drainage is needed, and in dry or well-drained ground the soil can be given additives to make the areas more water retentive. Alternatively, you can exploit such conditions by using plants that prefer them.

THE FUNCTIONAL PLAN

After you have analysed the plot, the next stage is to draw up a functional plan that indicates the position of the main areas in the garden. This is rather like putting together a jigsaw-puzzle, and both the site survey and analysis should be used, together with your list of requirements (as discussed in the *Garden Design* chapter).

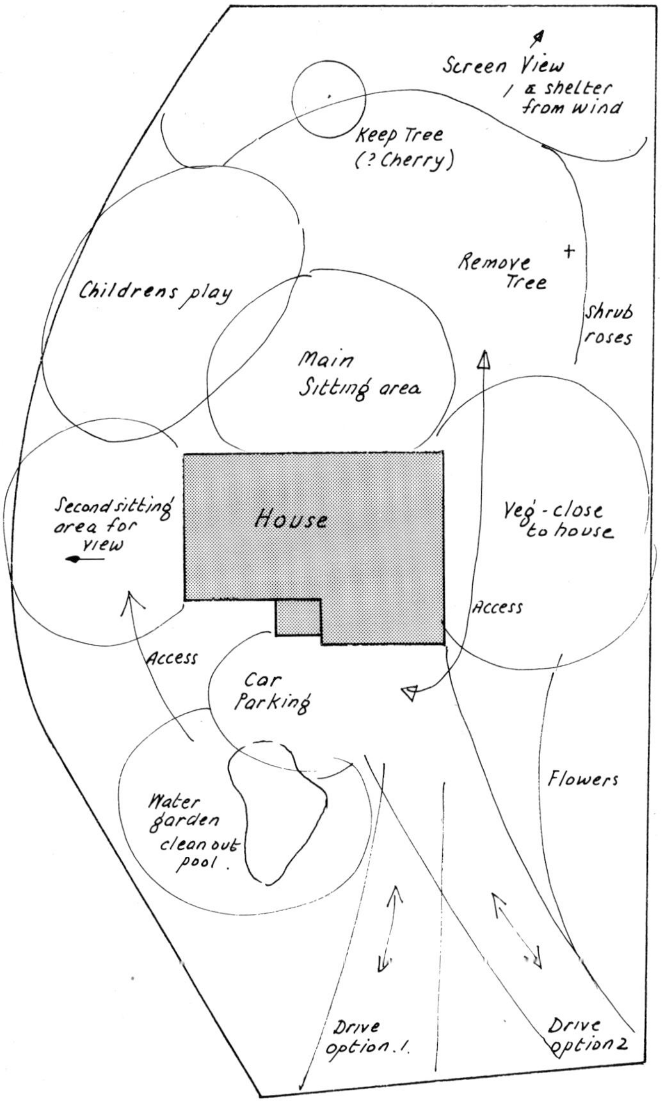

The best way to begin is by positioning the main seating area. If it is to be a terrace or patio near the house it is important to establish its position first because the garden will always seem to grow outwards from this point. Questions you should ask will include: Is this spot sunny enough and, if so, does the sun shine here too much? Is the position too noisy or windy and, if so, is there an alternative position that would be better? Can these problems be solved by building some sort of attractive shelter? How easy is it to gain access to and from the house?

Each proposed part of the garden, in terms of the role it will play, has to be similarly considered. This may mean endless moving about of ideas on paper so that eventually, as far as the plot will allow, each element occupies the ideal spot for its function. Walk around the garden picturing what it will be like to use the garden as you have planned it, assessing the feel and size of each area in relation to another.

You should end up with a roughly sketched-out plan broadly indicating where, for example, the vegetable garden, main sitting area, lawn and drive will be positioned. However, at this point leave the options open – for example, it might be necessary to have the drive coming up to the house slightly further to the right once the more detailed outline plan has been worked on. This is the next stage.

Screen View / a shelter from wind

Keep Tree (? Cherry)

Remove Tree

Shrub roses

Childrens play

Main Sitting area

Second sitting area for view

House

Veg - close to house

Access

Access

Car Parking

Flowers

Water garden clean out pool.

Drive option. 1.

Drive option 2

THE OUTLINE PLAN

The final design, showing in greater detail the positions and shapes of each element in the garden, can include anything from siting a mixed border, shrubbery and rose bed to showing the exact layout of a formal vegetable patch or a children's play space and placing an extra seating area to make the most of a good view.

When drawing up the outline plan, remember that, in three dimensions, perspective tends to bring elements closer together so that they may appear smaller at a distance. Perspective may dictate that certain elements need to be adjusted slightly when you come to make the garden. Avoid making major alterations since they may have repercussions on other parts of the design.

Whatever the combination of elements, they need to be put together in an harmonious way. The proportions should be relevant to their functions and the size of the garden, and in accordance with the principles of good garden design – as dealt with in detail in *Garden Design*. The *Garden Plans* chapter shows many examples of the way such elements can be put together to make successful gardens, and should help you to see how to draw up your own design.

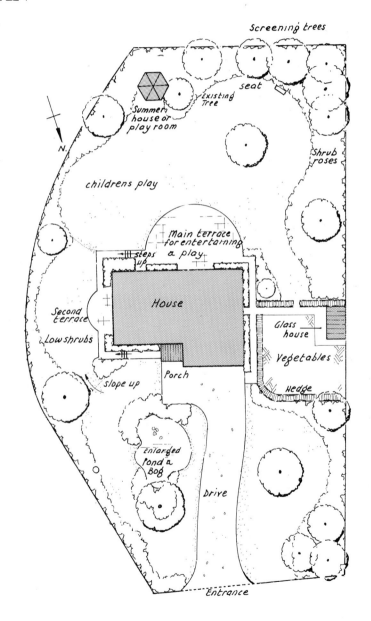

THE FINISHING TOUCHES

The main constituents of a garden's design and construction are usually referred to as 'hard' and 'soft' landscaping, the hard being the constructional items such as walling and paving, the soft meaning the planting, top soiling and turfing. In a new garden, the choice of hard materials can be appreciated instantly whereas the soft can take years to reach maturity. Because of this, unfortunately, gardens are mostly imbalanced for several years after construction, and little can be done about it except be patient.

Once the outline plan is complete, make photocopies or tracings of it and add the details of the hard and soft landscaping and the decorative elements and other practical items. Deal with each separately: for example, use one copy to note down all the constructions, their materials and details; use another to show a detailed planting plan indicating numbers of plants and their spacings: and on a third copy indicate the positioning of such 'extras' as statues and ornaments, a barbecue and lighting.

HARD LANDSCAPING

Walls, fences, paving and steps form an important part of the framework of the garden and the materials used need to be carefully considered. What effect is to be achieved? Is natural stone in keeping with the surroundings? Would brickwork be better? Is there to be a common theme to the materials used? How durable do the constructions need to be? It is essential to answer these questions and to think through all the requirements in advance of buying expensive materials.

Walls

Walls establish boundaries, provide shelter, screen and divide the garden into compartments. Of all the vertical elements, they tend to have the greatest influence on the overall appearance of a garden and can, in some circumstances, dictate style. They should be made of the strongest materials, and ideally, they should be provided with a coping – a water-resistant top – and damp-proof course.

In walls of **random natural stone**, there is no attempt made to organize the stones in horizontal rows, but corner stones need to be comparatively square, and to be regularly positioned, for stability. An attractive top course or coping style is called 'cocks and hens' where small and large pieces alternate in a castellated manner. **Thin natural stone** laid out horizontally provides a more linear feel. A suitable coping employs the same material selected for its uniformity of thickness, and the sides should extend a little beyond the faces of the wall for its protection.

Flint or pebbles make handsome walls, but because the shapes are small and irregular, squarish corner stones need to be used for stability. Bricks are an ideal material and can also be used to provide a firm base and coping. An additional feature can be created by a row of tiles positioned beneath the bricks in the coping.

Slate or very thin stone can make excellent decorative walls, particularly when used in attractive patterns such as herring-bone, in which each row of pieces, bounded by strong corner stones, leans left or right at an angle of about 30 degrees. The pattern can be used with mortar, or for dry stone walls in which no mortar is employed between the joints, and is best with a traditional decorative coping style.

Squared stone or imitation stone blocks made of concrete, cut to different lengths, can be used most attractively. A smooth coping with neat, regular sides looks most appropriate with this angular, regular shaped walling. Such a coping also suits **random rectangular stone**, holding together its more uneven arrangement. This type of walling uses blocks of all shapes and sizes, although they are all still basically rectangular. While it is quite difficult to achieve this pattern with natural stone (each piece has to be cut or sawn to shape), imitation blocks fit together easily, as they are usually cut based on multiples of, say 225mm (9in).

There are, of course, numerous patterns – bonds – that can be created from bricks. The strongest brick bond is known as the **English bond**. It alternates the header (end of the brick) and stretcher (side of the brick) faces with each row. A more complicated bond, and to my mind the most attractive, is the **Flemish bond**, which alternates the stretchers and headers on every row.

The **stretcher bond**, in which every brick is laid with the stretcher face outwards, is useful for low walls less than 75cm (2½ft) high, which are only 100mm (4in) thick.

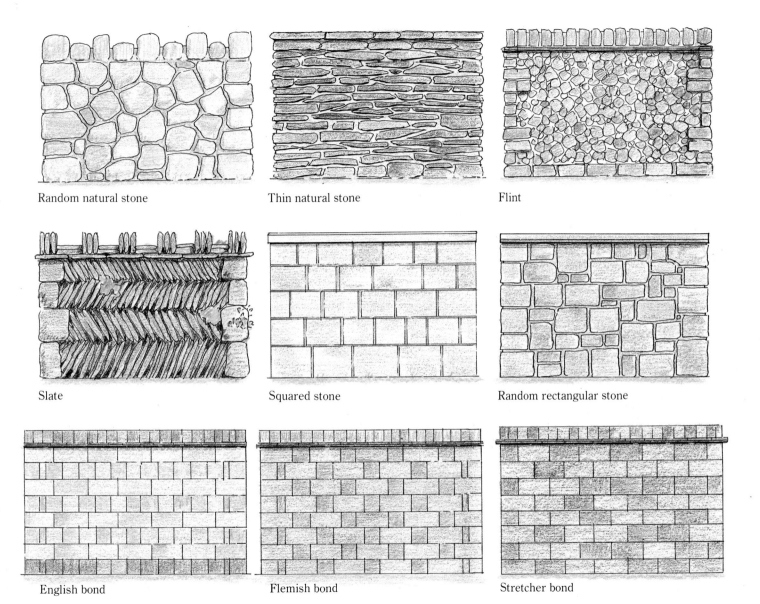

Random natural stone

Thin natural stone

Flint

Slate

Squared stone

Random rectangular stone

English bond

Flemish bond

Stretcher bond

There are three types of wall: load bearing (for example, house walls), free standing (for example, boundary walls) or retaining (for example, for raised beds), and each has its own particular and appropriate specifications. It is best to take professional advice about construction – particularly as to the depth and quality of foundations, which largely determine stability.

There are many different materials from which walls can be built, including natural stone (random stone pieces or stone cut to blocks in various sizes), concrete (shaped as blocks, bricks, imitation stone, poured and shuttered) and brick (in various patterns known as 'bonds'). The method of construction, the choice of building material and the way the mortar is finished all contribute to the wall's appearance, the effects ranging from the comparatively bland look of 'flush' joints to the positive shadow lines of recessed joints.

Fences

A generally less costly option than walls, fences have their own role to play in garden design. Like walls, they perform different functions – defining a boundary, enclosing a small space, providing shade and protecting the garden from winds – and their appearance can enhance the garden's character. Fences need to be well supported with properly embedded posts, preferably of hardwood or concrete, and any timber will need to be treated regularly with preservative or paint. Although less durable than walls, fences can make better windbreaks, filtering the wind rather than providing a solid barrier that deflects and then traps it so creating turbulence within the garden. They form the ideal surface against which to train plants, as supports for climbers can be fixed on to them quite easily. Fences come in a variety of materials and styles, some of which are illustrated here.

Panels of reed fencing set within sturdy frames make an unusual and stylish boundary for this modern garden. The fencing deliberately reflects and enhances the Oriental appearance, and its horizontal and soft vertical lines complement the contrasting diagonals of the wooden decking.

Fences

There are various styles of wooden fencing in ready-made panels, including **vertical close board**, in which the boards are often overlapped to make a really strong fence, and **interwoven wood**, which has vertical thin slats weaving between the horizontal slats. The best panels have a coping board at the top and a gravel board at the bottom which help to keep the wood ends dry.

Wattle fencing has a softer, rustic look. It is made of thin, pliable branches, either whole or split, that are woven together like basket work.

Post and rail fencing can be erected comparatively quickly and, although it does not protect against the elements, it defines a boundary well.

Palisade fencing makes an attractive high boundary in which palings (posts or strips) with rounded or pointed tops are screwed or nailed to horizontal rails. Made using the same principle, but with spaces between the poles and on a smaller scale, **picket** fencing gives a 'cottagey' feel to a low boundary and looks particularly charming with roses or clematis rambling over it.

A creative way to use fencing is by putting together different types of **trellis** panels to add interest to a view or boundary. You can achieve a *trompe l'oeil* effect, and enhance it with carefully trained plants.

Metal fences, whether wrought, cast iron or aluminium, come in many styles and are particularly appropriate for more formal garden designs and, especially, front gardens.

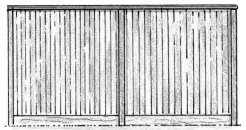
Vertical close board

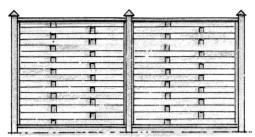
Interwoven wood

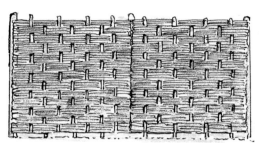
Wattle

Post and rail

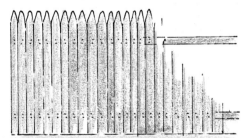
Palisade

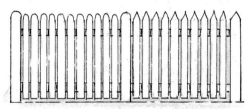
Picket

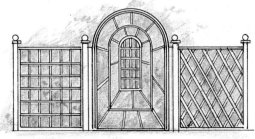
Trellis

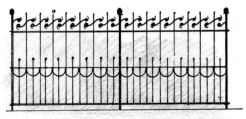
Metal

Paving

Paving has an important structural role in the garden, and should look attractive as well as being functional. It can be used for constructing all manner of areas, ranging from patios and parking spaces to paths and steps. Whatever the area, all paving materials should be sufficiently strong in three ways: to support the pressures of pedestrian and/or vehicular traffic; to resist wear caused by pedestrians and vehicles; and to resist the effects of weathering, especially frost in climates with cold winters. Unfortunately, not all materials are so tough, so it is worth getting expert advice to make sure that the materials you choose suit the conditions and the job they are required to do. Also, ensure that the surface is laid on an appropriate base since it is that which provides the support.

Like walls, paving can be made of natural stone, concrete and brick. However, there are other materials that can also be used such as tiles and paviours and, particularly for paths, gravel (especially the fine-grade self-binding type) and flexible materials like Tarmacadam and asphalt. Wood – if it is specially treated against rot and slipping – can make a range of attractive surfaces, from sawn-log stepping stones to raised timber decking.

Natural stone comes in a variety of forms ranging from square or rectangular shapes, which have been cut or sawn, to setts (blocks of hard stone such as granite), pebbles (either whole or halved) and random shapes, for use as crazy paving. Concrete, too, can be bought in square or shaped blocks and as bricks. All these come in a variety of finishes, as do paviours and tiles.

The choice of material, then, is almost endless and the ways in which paving can be laid is equally varied. A few examples are illustrated here. As well as making use of various combinations of pattern, the materials, of course, need not be used singly. Thus, a very wide range of potentially attractive ground patterns can be created.

Left Using old brick as a paving material imparts a mellow softness to any design. Here laid in a basket-weave pattern, it makes a perfect setting for this cottage herb garden.

Paving

The most informal paving style is a **random** design – sometimes called crazy paving – using natural stone or broken paving slabs. It is very useful for winding paths and – especially when laid in grass – seating areas in natural gardens.

Random rectangular paving, uses different-sized, roughly rectangular-shaped natural stone or concrete units made to resemble stone. It retains a soft, informal feel in a more ordered design.

More formal patterns include symmetrical **square** paving with unbroken joint lines running in each direction. It can be made of real stone or slate, although these are expensive when cut, or you can use concrete units in varying shades and textures, or even clay and ceramic tiles. A less severe design is the **basket weave** pattern, built up using pairs of bricks to make each square, and running north–south/east–west alternately.

Herring-bone is a lively design using brick in a zig-zag pattern. It can be laid either straight – with bricks running horizontally and vertically – thus fitting a rectangular or straight-sided shape, or diagonally, as shown here, in which case some framing is needed to keep small pieces in place.

Bricks can also be laid in the wall-like **stretcher bond** pattern, or the **stack bond** in which the bricks are 'stacked' in neat rows and columns. In both patterns the joints make unbroken lines along the long sides of the bricks, creating a sense of distance or breadth.

Another 'busy' pattern is **fishscale** – so-called because of its overlapping semi-circles – which can be achieved by using half-bricks, setts or specially made concrete units.

Hexagonal paving is a more static design, and makes a good patio surface. It is normally made with tiles or textured finished concrete slabs.

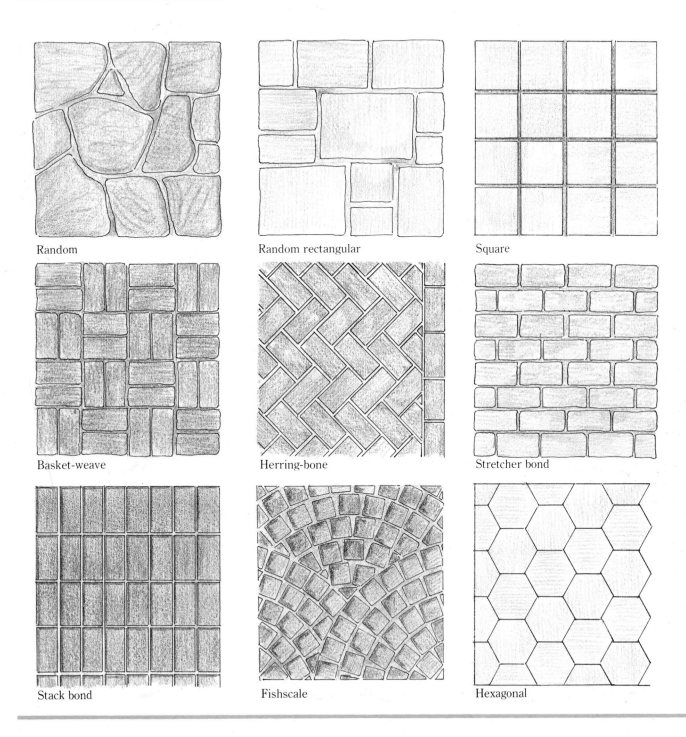

Random

Random rectangular

Square

Basket-weave

Herring-bone

Stretcher bond

Stack bond

Fishscale

Hexagonal

Steps

Steps, although usually created of the same materials as those used for paving, deserve special mention. They can be ornamental as well as functional and provide structural interest and possibly a sense of intrigue if used well. In addition, if well proportioned, they give breadth to a garden. Their styles can be appropriately formal, informal, even rustic; they can be square, rectangular, circular, zig-zagged, curved – don't feel you have to stick to conventions. Make the steps fit your requirements and not vice versa, but do ensure you stick to the basic principles of safe design.

Above all else, steps should be comfortable to ascend and descend. The slope of a flight of steps is known as the 'going' and this should never exceed 40 degrees from the horizontal, otherwise the steps appear intimidating going up and frightening going down. The minimum safe riser (the vertical part of the step) in a garden is 100mm (4in) – below this there is a likelihood of a person tripping – and the maximum is 200mm (8in). The tread should, if possible be about 300mm (12in) deep. A popular proportion for garden steps is a 150mm (6in) riser with a 375mm (15in) tread, but this is not always achievable. In general it is a good idea for the depth of the tread plus twice the height of the riser to be at least 600mm (2ft).

Tread and riser sizes should be constant throughout the flight and, ideally, at every ten to twelve steps a landing should be provided for a pause. In order to preserve the rhythm of gait, the landing depth should be the equivalent of two or three times the depth of the tread.

With stone or brick steps it is best if the tread projects slightly beyond the riser at the front to create a shadow line. Not only is this visually pleasing but it helps to define the steps more clearly in poor light. Similarly, hand rails or side walls that are aesthetically pleasing can be built beside the steps for safety.

When designing steps, bear these aspects in mind but also remember that steps take up more room than is generally supposed. For example, a mere six steps each of which is 1.8m (6ft) wide with treads 450mm (18in) deep will account for 4.8m² (54sqft). Depending upon their position in the plot this could extend well into an area and in a small garden, in particular, they could take up a very significant proportion of the garden.

Above *Simple wooden steps blend in perfectly with the dramatic jungly foliage lining this stairway. They make an exciting and mysterious passage to a half-hidden upper level. Care needs to be taken if wood is used as a material for steps; it needs treating against rot and should be given an anti-slip finish for safety.*

DECORATIVE ELEMENTS AND EFFECTS

In most gardens it is important to have ornamental elements in the design. They can of course be planned to be partially hidden to be enjoyed for their own sake, but they are especially important for acting as focal points – as an integral part of the structure and composition of the garden. Whether they are works of art or functional items that are at the same time ornamental, they should be in keeping with, and harmonize with, the garden as a whole. Suiting its style and size wherever possible, they should be part of the original design, but a garden's form should never be so rigid that minor additions or subtractions cannot be made later. Beware of upsetting the balance at a later date, though, for an ill-chosen object can do this all too easily.

Ornaments that are of informative interest make lively focal points. Items like sundials, telescopes, carved stone or plaques and chess sets often work particularly well in a garden, perhaps because each calls for a positive response from the beholder. Statues, urns and fountains are excellent for quieter contemplation. Many more functional items such as seats, tables, barbecues, pergolas, conservatories, drinking fountains or pots can at the same time be ornamental. (Indeed they should be if they are permanently visible in the garden.)

Left *A sundial on a handsome pedestal is thoroughly in keeping in size and in style with the dignified atmosphere of this traditional garden. This kind of ornament looks best situated as a terminal focal point, or at the centre of a garden composition as here, where it is the focus of the surrounding bed and the decorative tiled path.*

A pergola is an important garden structure, and its construction and materials affect the look of the whole garden. Supporting piers of brick or stone need good-sized cross-members to be in scale (above left); they make a solid edifice, excellent for heavy climbers such as wisteria. Wooden uprights with slimmer beams (above right) make an airier, elegant construction, perfect for lighter climbers such as roses.

Pergolas deserve a special mention as they make such delightful additions to any garden. On maturity, they provide tunnels of flowers and greenery that are enhanced by the tapestry of light and shade within the frame. It is important that the size of the pergola is appropriate to its intended use as well as its setting. If you plan to grow plants with long racemes of flowers, take this into account – the pergola will need to be sufficiently high to avoid uncomfortable collisions. The width is important too and should if possible allow at least two people walking side by side to pass beneath – they are the perfect location for strolling.

Since a pergola will generally carry a considerable weight, its supports and cross-beams need to be strong and well built. Bricks are the ideal material for the columns and timber should be used for the beams. However, timber columns suitably treated with preservative, are strong and have the added advantage of being cheaper.

Lighting

Lighting adds another facet to a garden, extending its life and use in the evenings, and is best planned from the beginning. A well-designed lighting scheme can entirely transform the appearance of a garden at night, altering its character by bringing dramatic or subtle use of light and shade into play. A path lit by pools of light offers a soft, illuminating effect, intriguing the eye, or the view of a floodlit patio can be enhanced with lights nestling among pots of flowers and surrounding beds.

Focal points can be illuminated, but remember that subtlety is all-important. It is very easy to overdo lighting which then looks harsh and vulgar. Equally, as with every other element in the garden, light fittings must be appropriate and in harmony with the garden style.

Some light fittings are ornamental, others should be concealed within planting or at the side of walls or steps. There are companies that specialize in garden lighting and if the intention is to make great use of this element it may be best to employ one. But whatever you decide to do – and there is a wide range of fittings and lamps available – do make sure that they are wired up by a qualified lighting engineer.

Lighting is of particular importance when, as in this small garden, the plot is designed to be an outdoor room for relaxation and entertaining as well as somewhere to grow and display plants. Even if using the garden at night is not the most important consideration, the simplest lighting system can make the garden look good from the house after dark. It brings out different aspects of the garden, accentuating the shape, form and silhouettes of plants and garden features and dramatizing leaf shapes and unfamiliar contours.

SOFT LANDSCAPING

On the outline plan, you will probably have marked planting areas simply as 'mixed border' or 'old-fashioned rose bed', but now is the time to work out appropriate schemes, pinpointing which plants are needed where, and how many. You will usually have to refer to gardening reference books and good catalogues and note down colours, cultural requirements and planting distances. It is best to write the names of plants on the plan so that you have an instant visual reference. Touches of colour, too, help to differentiate between one area and another. It may be easier if you can use a copy of the outline plan, or parts of it that have been enlarged to scale. It is often not possible to write hundreds of plant names on a drawing that may well have been appropriate for outlining but is too small for detail.

First, you need to place the large, permanent plants, such as trees and shrubs, that provide a good structural basis; then, work downwards to the smallest plants, remembering to space them all correctly. Colour and flowering times should obviously be borne in mind as you do this, since these aspects will influence the atmosphere of the garden.

When noting down the plants on the plan with their quantities it is a good idea to list them separately as well; this is by far the easiest way to place orders with various nurseries when the time has come.

Right *This garden shows a marvellous juxtaposition of dramatic clumps of rounded leaf forms against more feathery foliage and tall spikes with bright accents of flower colour; this is set perfectly against the foil of an expanse of green hedge enlivened by trees with lighter green and coppery leaves.*

A careful design will take the height and shape of plants and their foliage into account as well as planning for flower colour, and it is important to try to envisage the grown plants in three-dimensions when drawing the plan.

Left *It is also important to plan carefully for colour effects. Here the stunning tonal effect of the clump of pink* Diascia rigescens *is perfectly offset and echoed by the pale pink of the paeonies behind.*

COMPLETING THE PLAN

Once you have put all the relevant detail on the plan it becomes a valuable document. You should protect and store it after taking several copies of it, using these for the field work since plan copies soon become faded, torn or dirty in the garden. Copies should also be taken to nurseries for advice or reference. Perhaps you will consult a contractor to carry out some of the work, so he or she will need copies for pricing.

Once you feel that the plan is finalized, it can be well worth inking it in. This really does make it permanent and it should last for years. You may be surprised how often you need to refer back to the original, especially if you have planned to realize the project over several years.

Realizing the plan

The plan is the first but vital step towards the creation of a beautiful and functional garden and it is hoped that you will derive a great deal of pleasure from preparing it. However, it really is only the beginning. Just as it was important to work through many stages in an organized manner to reach this point, it is equally important to work out a strategy when realizing the plan.

The first question to ask is: How much of the implementation am I prepared to do, have I time to do so, and most importantly, am I competent to do so? Building walls and terraces and cultivation and planting require skill and knowledge. The results of ignorance could be disastrous and it might well be worth using the services of a specialist landscape contractor, particularly for some of the building and construction work.

So, decide on what work can be done without help and what can't. Then plan the logistics of the operation and draw up a timetable; it is best to make sure that the work coincides with the appropriate seasons.

For a completely new garden, a logical sequence of operations would run as follows:

1 Site clearance (protect any trees and plants retained).
2 Land forming (first remove top soil for later replacement).
3 Marking out the borders and other areas using canes and string or the environment-friendly paint sprays that are now available (2 and 3 are interchangeable depending on the circumstances).
4 Laying foundations for walls.
5 Constructing the walls.
6 Laying foundations for paving, including front drive.
7 Laying the paving (except front drive).
8 Top soiling, or top soil replacement.
9 Preparing the soil for planting.
10 Installation of lighting and, in hot climates, irrigation systems.
11 Planting.
12 Preparation of proposed grassed areas.
13 Sowing grass or turfing.
14 Completion of front drive.
15 Cleaning up and final touches.

Work should begin at the rear of a house (if access is via the front) and then continue in such a way as to ensure that work already done is not damaged by pedestrians or vehicular traffic having to pass over it to reach uncompleted areas. Thus, work usually continues at the sides, and the front garden is left untouched almost until last.

If a contractor is employed, do take up references and check credentials. Preferably engage a person (or organization) who belongs to a recognized trade, professional group or association. It is usually better to get quotations that are a fixed price rather than an estimate. Check, too, that the operator is fully insured.

PLANNING
FOR PLANTS

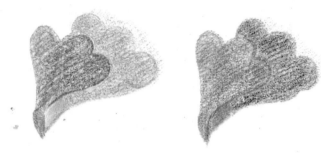

When choosing the planting to fill your garden, it is important to think about which plants will do best in the conditions existing in your garden, and which will suit your individual preferences. This chapter gives a selection of plants suitable for particular sites – for example in dry sunny conditions or open exposed areas – and for special purposes, such as for those who want a low-maintenance garden or who love roses.

Examples of coloured plans for borders using these plants show how they can be combined in such sites. Harmonious and contrasting colour effects are explained, and further border plans give suggestions for particularly effective colour combinations.

PLANT HARDINESS

In the lists that follow, numbers in brackets are hardiness zone ratings, giving an approximate minimum temperature a plant will tolerate in winter. Most parts of the British Isles are in zone 8, the coldest northern areas being in zone 7, while the mildest areas around the southern and western coasts are zone 9. However, your local climatic conditions, which may differ from the general area, can influence a plant's hardiness, as can a range of other factors including its original geographic source.

Because it is more difficult to specify the limits of cold tolerance of herbaceous plants and bulbs, hardiness zones have not been detailed; instead, an asterisk (*) marks plants that are known not to be hardy throughout the British Isles, Europe and the United States of America, and genera marked like this contain some members that are not hardy throughout these areas.

Some plants are particularly versatile, and may be found listed here under more than one set of conditions.

Hardiness zones showing the approximate range of average annual minimum temperatures

1	below −45°C/−50°F
2	−45°C/−50°F to −40°C/−40°F
3	−40°C/−40°F to −34°C/−30°F
4	−34°C/−30°F to −29°C/−20°F
5	−29°C/−20°F to −23°C/−10°F
6	−23°C/−10°F to −18°C/0°F
7	−18°C/0°F to −12°C/10°F
8	−12°C/10°F to −7°C/20°F
9	−7°C/20°F to −1°C/30°F
10	−1°C/30°F to 4°C/40°F

DRY SUNNY SITES

The following plants are relatively drought-resistant and will thrive in full sun, although all will grow better if not subjected to prolonged drought. Plants with narrow, needle-like leaves, grey foliage or succulent leaves are naturally suited to these conditions; those with very broad foliage are unlikely to thrive and some variegated foliage may scorch.

A dry, sunny site enclosed by walls and preferably sheltered from the morning sun in winter provides the most favoured position for growing plants that would be too tender for more exposed parts of the garden. Such microclimates can be exploited by adventurous gardeners to try plants from warmer hardiness zones.

Trees

Cercis siliquastrum (7)
Cladrastis lutea (3)
Eucalyptus (7–9)
Gleditsia triacanthos (3)
Morus nigra (7)
Pyrus salicifolia 'Pendula' (5)
Quercus ilex (8)
Robinia × *ambigua* and

R. pseudoacacia (3)
Sophora japonica (5)

Shrubs

Artemisia arborescens 'Faith Raven' and 'Powis Castle' (8)
Berberis thunbergii (5)
Buddleja davidii (6)
Caryopteris (8)
Ceanothus (5–9)
Cistus (7–8)
Clerodendrum trichotomum (6)
Cytisus (6–9)
Elaeagnus angustifolia caspina (3) and *E. commutata* (2)
Hibiscus syriacus (6)
Lavandula (6–9)
Lavatera thuringiaca cvs. (inc. *L.* 'Olbia Rosea') (8)
Perovskia atriplicifolia and hybrids (6)
Phlomis anatolica and *P. fruticosa* (8)
Rhus typhina laciniata (3)
Romneya (8)
Sambucus racemosa 'Plumosa Aurea' (5)
Santolina (6–7)
Senecio (shrubby) (now *Brachyglottis*) eg *monroi, compactus,* 'Sunshine' (8)
Spartium junceum (8)
Syringa (2–7)

A dry sunny border

Left *In a dry sunny border you have a choice between silver foliage and softly coloured flowers (lavender,* Santolina *and* Cistus) *or bold, bright tones (salvias, penstemons and* Zauschneria). *Grassy or spiky foliage of iris and lily relatives provide effective foliage contrast. This plan combines the best of both sorts. Even the most drought-tolerant plants may need watering until they are established.*

Climbers and Wall Plants
Buddleja crispa (8)
B. fallowiana (8)
Cytisus battandieri (8)
Lonicera (3–8)
Solanum crispum
   'Glasnevin' (8)
Vitex agnus-castus (7)
Vitis (5–8)

Herbaceous and border plants
*Acanthus spinosus**
Achillea
*Agapanthus**
Alstroemeria ligtu hybrids
Anthemis tinctoria
Centaurea
*Crocosmia**
Dianthus
Dictamnus albus
Echinops ritro ruthenicus
*Eryngium**
*Euphorbia characias wulfenii**
Iris bearded cvs.
Lychnis coronaria
Nepeta × faassenii
Oenothera biennis
*Penstemon**
Phygelius aequalis
   and *P. × rectus**
Salvia × superba
   and *S. × sylvestris*
Stachys byzantina
Zauschneria (now correctly
   Epilobium canum)*

MOIST SUNNY SITES
Although many of the following plants will not tolerate water-logging, all are at their best in constantly moist positions. Leaf size need not be limited by availability of water and so foliage effect can be boldly architectural or in some cases lush and almost tropical.

Trees
Aesculus (3–8)
Carya (5–9)
Cercidiphyllum japonicum (5)
Eucryphia (8–9)
Juglans (5–9)
Liquidambar styraciflua (6)
Magnolia (5–9)
Malus (2–9)
Nyssa sylvatica (3)
Platanus (5–9)
Prunus (3–9)
Salix alba sericea (2)
Sorbus (2–7)

Shrubs
Acer Japanese maples (6)
Cornus alba cvs. (2)
Fuchsia (8–10)
Hypericum (5–10)
Kalmia (2–7)
Philadelphus (5–9)
Potentilla (2–4)
Viburnum (3–9)

Climbers and wall plants
Actinidia (5–7)
Clematis (4–9)
Jasminum officinale (7–8)
Wisteria (5–9)

Herbaceous and border plants
Aconitum
Anemone × hybrida
Ajuga
Alchemilla mollis
Aquilegia
Aster
Astilbe
Astrantia
Brunnera macrophylla
Campanula
*Cortaderia**
*Cynara**
Filipendula
Geranium (*)
Hemerocallis
Hosta, blue-leaved
   and *H. plantaginea*
Iris sibirica
*Kniphofia**
*Lobelia × speciosa**
Macleaya
Miscanthus
Nierembergia repens
Paeonia
Phlox maculata
   and *P. paniculata*

TOTAL SHADE
In total shade plants not only receive no direct sunlight but are completely overshadowed by a canopy of trees or by buildings. Here plants receive only a small fraction of the light they would in an open situation shaded from direct sun.

Total shade is perhaps the most difficult and limiting situation for garden plants, particularly as such areas are usually very dry. Even with regular watering, these plants are likely to be very slow to establish because low light levels retard growth. You can make the sombre appearance of such areas less gloomy by incorporating forms of plants on the list with variegated or golden foliage and pale flowers.

Trees
Ilex × altaclarensis
   and *I. aquifolium* (7–8)
Taxus baccata (6–7)

Shrubs
Aucuba (7)
bamboos (some) (5–10)
Buxus (6–8)
Camellia (7–9)
Cephalotaxus (6–7)
Cornus canadensis (2)

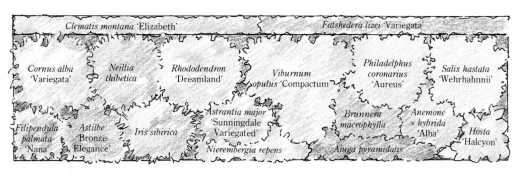

A moist sunny border

Left A moist sunny site offers few limitations and provides the opportunity of indulging in the biggest, boldest and most extravagantly architectural foliage. More restraint may be preferred, particularly near the house; this border plan provides ample interest from foliage form and flower colour throughout the growing season.

Daphne laureola (7)
and *D. pontica* (6)
Elaeagnus (evergreen) (6–8)
Euonymus fortunei (5)
Fatsia japonica (7)
Gaultheria (6–10)
Hypericum calycinum (5–6)
Ilex (some) (3–10)
Leucothoë fontanesiana (5)
Ligustrum (many) (3–9)
Lonicera pileata (6)
and *L. nitida* (7–8)
Mahonia aquifolium (5)
Osmanthus heterophyllus
and *O. decorus* (7)
Pachysandra terminalis (5)
Podocarpus (8–10)
Prunus laurocerasus
and *P. lusitanica* (7)
Rhododendron Hardy Hybrids
(6–8)
Rubus (some) (5–8)
Ruscus (7–9)
Sarcococca (6–9)
Skimmia (7–9)
Symphoricarpos (2–9)
Taxus (2–9)
Viburnum davidii (7–8)

Climbers
Lapageria rosea (9)
Lonicera japonica 'Halliana' (5)
Parthenocissus (3–9)
Pileostegia viburnoides (9)

Herbaceous and Border Plants
*Asarum**
Athyrium filix-femina
*Bergenia**
Convallaria
Dicentra
Digitalis purpurea
Dryopteris
Polystichum
Epimedium
Euphorbia amygdaloides rubra
and *E. a. robbiae*
Galium odoratum
Geranium phaeum,
G. maculatum, G. nodosum
and *G. macrorrhizum*
Helleborus foetidus
and *H. orientalis*
Hosta
*Liriope**
Milium effusum aureum
Phyllitis
Polygonatum
Polystichum
Rodgersia
Saxifraga fortunei, S. stolonifera
and *S. × urbium**
Smilacina
Tellima
Tiarella
Tolmiea
*Tricyrtis**
Vancouveria
Vinca
Viola labradorica purpurea

DRY SHADY SITES
These conditions are typical of many town gardens and of areas partly overshadowed by trees, and the range of suitable plants is much smaller than for sun or moist shade. Few brightly coloured flowers will thrive here. This is perhaps just as well: whites and pale pastel colours are particularly telling in such positions. Although mature plants of the following will continue to flourish, it will probably be necessary to water new plantings, at least for their first season.

Trees
Ailanthus altissima (5)
Betula (2–7)
Crataegus (4–7)
Ilex × altaclarensis
and *I. aquifolium* (7–8)
Sorbus aucuparia (2)
Taxus baccata (6–7)

Shrubs
Amelanchier (3–6)
Aucuba japonica (7)
Buxus (6–8)
Danaë racemosa (7)
Fatsia japonica (7)
Euonymus japonicus (8)
Ilex (3–10)
Ligustrum japonicum (8)

and *L. ovalifolium* (6)
Pittosporum tenuifolium (9)
Pleioblastus variegatus (syn.
Arundinaria variegata) (7)
Prunus laurocerasus (7)
Rubus tricolor (7–8)
Ruscus aculeatus (7)
Sambucus nigra (6)
Sarcococca (6–9)

Climbers and wall plants
× *Fatshedera lizei* (8)
Hedera (5–9)
Parthenocissus (3–9)

Herbaceous and border plants
*Acanthus mollis**
Alchemilla mollis
*Bergenia**
Digitalis purpurea
and *D. grandiflora*
Dryopteris
Euphorbia amygdaloides rubra
and *E. a. robbiae*
Geranium (some)*
Helleborus foetidus, H. niger
and *H. orientalis*
Iris foetidissima
Lamium
*Liriope**
Polygonatum
Polystichum
Vancouveria
Vinca
Waldsteinia

A dry shady border

Left *Grey foliage plants are not usually tolerant of shade but the preponderance of dark green leaved plants suited to a dry shady border can be leavened by including some variegated or gold foliage and pale flowers. Watering may be needed, particularly if the house shelters the border from rain.*

MOIST SHADY SITES

Damper soil allows larger leaves and bolder foliage effects. There are a great many plants which revel in these conditions, although again the paler colours are often the most effective.

Trees
Ailanthus altissima (5)
Betula nigra (5)
  and *B. pendula* (2)
Prunus padus (4)
Sorbus aucuparia (2)

Shrubs
Acer Japanese maples (6)
bamboos (most) (5–10)
Camellia (7–9)
Cassiope (2–5)
Cephalotaxus (6–7)
Cornus alba
  and *C. canadensis* (2)
Fatsia japonica (7)
Gaultheria (3–9)
Hydrangea (5–9)
Ilex (3–10)
Leucothoë (5–9)
Mahonia (5–10)
Pieris (5–7)
Podocarpus (8–10)
Rhododendron (3–10)
Skimmia (7–9)
Vaccinium (2–10)

Climbers and wall plants
Hydrangea petiolaris (5)
Lonicera japonica 'Halliana' (5)
Parthenocissus (3–9)
Pileostegia (9)

Herbaceous and border plants
Actaea
Ajuga
Alchemilla
Aruncus
*Asarum**
Astilbe
Astilboides (formerly *Rodgersia tabularis*)
*Bergenia**
Brunnera
Cimicifuga
Dicentra
Epimedium
Gentiana asclepiadea
Geranium (some)*
× *Heucherella*
Helleborus niger
  and *H. orientalis*
Hosta
Kirengeshoma
*Ligularia**
Omphalodes
*Ophiopogon**
Phlox maculata
Polygonatum
*Primula**
Pulmonaria
Rheum
Rodgersia
Saxifraga fortunei, S. × *urbium*
  and *S. stolonifera**
Smilacina
Symphytum
Tellima
Tiarella
Tolmiea menziesii
Trachystemon orientalis
Trillium
Uvularia
Vancouveria
Viola (some)
Waldsteinia

SEASIDE AREAS

Seaside climates differ from those inshore in a number of ways that affect the range of plants that can be grown: winds tend to be stronger and salt-laden but temperatures are less extreme because of the equalizing effect of the sea; increased ultraviolet light helps ripen the wood of some plants that would not be hardy inland. As a result, seaside gardens have their own characteristic range of wind-firm, salt-tolerant plants, many of them chosen to thrive on neglect in the gardens of holiday homes.

Trees
Arbutus unedo (8)
Crataegus (1–7)
Cupressus macrocarpa (8)
Eucalyptus (7–9)
Fraxinus (3–9)
Griselinia littoralis (8)
Pinus nigra maritima (4),
  P. radiata (7)
  and *P. muricata* (8)
Quercus ilex (8)
  and *Q. robur* (5)
Salix (most) (1–10)
Sorbus aucuparia (2)
  and *S. aria* (6)

Shrubs
Atriplex halimus (8)
Berberis darwinii (7)
Buddleja davidii (6)
Ceanothus (5–9)
Choisya ternata (8)
Cistus (7–8)
Cordyline (8–9)
Cotoneaster (many) (3–8)
Elaeagnus × *ebbingei* (6),
  E. glabra (8)
  and *E. pungens* (7)
Escallonia (most) (7–9)
Euonymus fortunei (5)
Fuchsia (8–10)
Genista (most) (5–9)
Hebe (6–9)
Hippophaë rhamnoides (3)
Hydrangea macrophylla (5–6)

A moist shady border

Left *Although many plants that revel in moist shady conditions such as astilbes and ligularias have brash, bright flowers, the softer, paler colours used here with variegated foliage will illuminate a shady border in a much more pleasing way. The pure blue of gentians and* Omphalodes *appears much more vibrant out of direct sunlight.*

Lavandula (6–9)
Olearia (most) (7–9)
Phillyrea angustifolia (9)
Phlomis (most) (8–10)
Phormium (8–10)
Rosmarinus officinalis (7–9)
Salvia officinalis
Santolina (6–7)
Tamarix (2–9)
Viburnum (2–9)

Climbers and wall plants
Garrya elliptica (9)
Polygonum aubertii
  and *P. baldschuanicum* (5)

Herbaceous and border plants
*Agapanthus**
Anemone × *hybrida*
Armeria
*Cortaderia**
*Crocosmia**
*Erigeron**
*Eryngium**
Iris bearded cvs.
*Kniphofia**
Nepeta mussinii
  and *N.* × *faassenii*
*Sedum**

OPEN EXPOSED SITES
In winter, plants in exposed sites suffer more wind damage, more frost penetration and more desiccation when frozen; in summer, they are more subject to drought. Only the toughest species will tolerate such conditions, many of them exactly the same plants we associate with such sites in the wild. The following plants are suitable for exposed situations, although establishing some shelter will make it possible to grow a wider range of plants more successfully.

Trees
Acer pseudoplatanus (6)
Betula (most) (2–7)
Crataegus monogyna (5)
Fagus sylvatica (5)
Fraxinus excelsior (3)
Laburnum (5–9)
Larix decidua (2)
Pinus nigra maritima (4),
  P. sylvestris (3)
  and *P. radiata* (7)
Quercus robur (5)

Sorbus aucuparia (2)
  and *S. aria* (6)
Taxus baccata (6–7)
Tilia cordata (3–7)
Tsuga canadensis (5)

Shrubs
Berberis thunbergii (5)
Calluna vulgaris (5)
Cornus alba (2)
Corylus maxima (5)
Cotinus coggygria (5)
Cotoneaster horizontalis (5–6)
Daboecia (6–8)
Deutzia × *rosea* (6)
Elaeagnus commutata (2)
Erica carnea (6)
Euonymus fortunei (5)
  and *E. japonicus* (8)
Gaultheria shallon (6)
Hippophaë rhamnoides (3)
Hydrangea paniculata (3)
Juniperus communis
  and *J.* × *media* (3)
Kerria japonica (5)
Mahonia aquifolium (5)
Pachysandra terminalis (5)
Pernettya mucronata (7)
Philadelphus (many) (5–9)
Pieris floribunda (5)

Potentilla (2–4)
Rhododendron ponticum (6),
  R. Hardy Hybrids (6–8)
  and *R. yakushimanum* (5)
Salix (1–10)
Spiraea (3–9)
Tamarix (2–9)
Ulex (6–9)
Viburnum opulus (3)

Herbaceous and border plants
Achillea (shorter cvs.)
Alchemilla
Anaphalis
Anemone × *hybrida*
Armeria
Aster (shorter cvs.)
*Bergenia**
Centaurea
Echinops
*Eryngium**
*Geranium**
Hemerocallis
*Kniphofia**
Malva
Nepeta
Phalaris arundinacea 'Picta'
Potentilla
Scabiosa

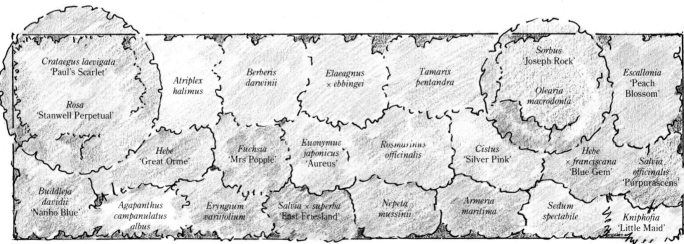

A seaside border

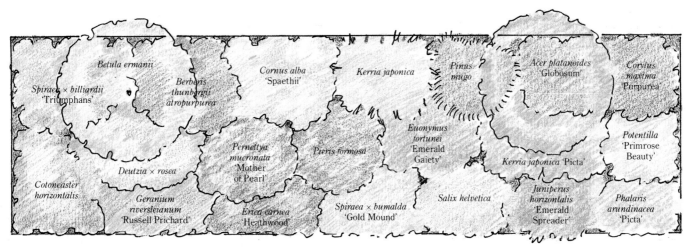

Betula ermanii · Spiraea × billiardii 'Triumphans' · Berberis thunbergii atropurpurea · Cornus alba 'Spaethii' · Kerria japonica · Pinus mugo · Acer platanoides 'Globosum' · Corylus maxima 'Purpurea' · Pernettya mucronata 'Mother of Pearl' · Pieris formosa · Euonymus fortunei 'Emerald Gaiety' · Potentilla 'Primrose Beauty' · Deutzia × rosea · Kerria japonica 'Picta' · Cotoneaster horizontalis · Geranium riversleianum 'Russell Prichard' · Erica carnea 'Heathwood' · Spiraea × bumalda 'Gold Mound' · Salix helvetica · Juniperus horizontalis 'Emerald Spreader' · Phalaris arundinacea 'Picta'

An open exposed border

Above *All gardens in exposed positions will benefit from the provision of some sort of shelter to filter the wind, whether it is a shelter belt of tough trees and shrubs or a slatted or pierced screen; a solid screen, hedge or belt is seldom a help and may either topple or cause severe problems from wind turbulence. With this proviso, the plants in this plan, many of them from exposed habitats in the wild, should all thrive in the most inhospitable site.*

Left *This border of plants that will tolerate salt spray and the buffeting of coastal gales includes many that would be markedly less hardy inland. As for most plants suited to seaside conditions, the colour range is mainly pinks, purples and blues.*

WATER OR BOG GARDENS

All of the following plants like to grow constantly within reach of water, by the side of a pond or stream or in a bog, although not all of them will tolerate their rootstock remaining submerged. Many are exuberantly and architecturally leafy, making such gardens among the most interesting for foliage effect. Although a large proportion will tolerate shade, flower colours are predominantly strong, including tints of yellow, orange, red and pink.

Trees
Alnus (2–7)
Betula pendula (2)
   and *B. nigra* (5)
Magnolia virginiana (5–10)
Metasequoia glyptostroboides (5)
Populus (2–9)
Pterocarya (6–7)
Quercus palustris (5)
Salix (1–10)
Taxodium (5–9)

Shrubs
Aronia (3–5)
Clethra (3–9)
Cornus alba
   and *C. stolonifera* (2)
Salix (1–10)
Symphoricarpos (2–9)

Herbaceous plants
*Arundo donax**
Astilbe
Caltha
Cardamine pratensis 'Flore
   Pleno'
Carex (some)
Darmera (syn. *Peltiphyllum*)
Euphorbia griffithii, E. palustris
   and *E. sikkimensis*
Filipendula
Geum rivale
*Gunnera**
Hosta
Houttuynia
Iris ensata, I. laevigata,
   I. pseudacorus and *I. sibirica*
*Libertia grandiflora**
*Ligularia**
Lysichiton
Lythrum
Matteuccia
*Mimulus**

Onoclea
Osmunda
Primula
Rheum
Rodgersia
Saururus cernuus
Scrophularia auriculata
   'Variegata'
Senecio smithii
Trollius
*Zantedeschia**

Submerged and aquatic plants
(Plants that grow with their rootstock below water.)
Aponogeton distachyos
Butomus umbellatus
Hottonia palustris
*Nymphaea**
Orontium aquaticum
Pontederia cordata
Sagittaria
Scirpus palustris
*Typha**

ROSES

Roses are welcome in any garden, both for their own sake and as essential ingredients in planting schemes. Although the stiff habit and fierce colour of some modern cultivars do not always lend themselves to mixed planting, the following varieties, most of them repeat flowering, are among the best of the old and the new sorts and should mix happily with other plants.

Shrub roses

'Alba Maxima'
Austin's "English roses" eg 'Graham Thomas'
'Celeste'
× *centifolia* 'Muscosa'
'Complicata'
'Comte de Chambord'
'Duchesse de Montebello'
'Félicité Parmentier'
'Frühlingsgold'
gallica 'Versicolor'
glauca (syn. *R. rubrifolia*)
Hybrid Musks eg 'Autumn Delight', 'Ballerina', 'Buff Beauty', 'Cordelia', 'Penelope', 'Prosperity'
'Jacques Cartier'
'James Veitch'
'Madame Isaac Pereire'
moyesii 'Geranium'
'Nevada'
× *odorata* 'Mutabilis' (syn. *R. chinensis* 'M.')
Rugosa Hybrids eg 'Blanc Double de Coubert', 'Fru Dagmar Hastrup', 'Roseraie de l'Hay'
'Stanwell Perpetual'
'The Fairy'
'Tuscany Superb'
'Variegata di Bologna'

Bush roses

Hybrid Tea, Floribunda, Polyantha Pompon and bush China roses of relatively modest growth can be used in the mixed border. Some are not reliably hardy, particularly old cultivars with much Tea rose in their parentage.
'Archiduc Joseph'
'Comtesse Vandal'
'Escapade'
'Europeana'
'Francis Dubreuil'
'Gruss an Aachen'
'Iceberg'
'Irène Watts'
'Lady Sylvia'
'Lavender Pinocchio'
'Lilli Marlene'
'Little White Pet'
'Madame Butterfly'
'Madame Louis Laperrière'
'Magenta'
'Margaret Merril'
'Michèle Meilland'
'Mrs Oakley Fisher'
'Nathalie Nypels'
'News'
'Old Blush China'
'Ophelia'
'Rosemary Rose'
'Sir Frederick Ashton'
'White Wings'

Climbing and rambler roses

The following list includes varieties of different heights suitable for walls or to cover structures such as pergolas, pillars or trelliswork. Varieties should be chosen for their intended site: vigorous sorts with very long stems such as 'Alexandre Girault' can be used to cover large structures or high walls but would be quite unsuitable for pillars only 2m/7ft high or trained against walls.

'Albéric Barbier'
'Albertine'
'Alchemist'
'Alexandre Girault'
banksiae
'Bleu Magenta'
brunonii 'La Mortola'
'Caroline Testout, Climbing'
'Constance Spry'
'Débutante'
'Easlea's Golden Rambler'
'Félicité Perpetué'
'François Juranville'
'Guinée'
'Iceberg, Climbing'
'Lady Hillingdon, Climbing'
'Madame Alfred Carrière'
'Madame Grégoire Staechelin'
'Madame Plantier'
'Mrs F. W. Flight'
'New Dawn'
'Parade'
'Phyllis Bide'
'Sanders' White Rambler'

Roses to grow into trees

Some roses do not lend themselves to being trained tidily against a wall; their natural grace is apparent only if they are allowed to tumble unrestrictedly through the branches of a tree. Such varieties can be used to add interest to an old and rather dull holly or yew, the dark foliage providing a telling contrast with the pale flowers of the rose; elderly and unproductive fruit trees will also act as a suitable host – but beware the most vigorous sorts which may completely smother such supports and cause their premature collapse.
'Adélaïde d'Orléans'
'Alchemist'
'Bobbie James'
filipes 'Kiftsgate'
'Lykkefund'
'New Dawn'

'Paul's Himalayan Musk'
'Princesse Marie'
'Rambling Rector'
'Splendens' ('Ayrshire Splendens')
'Wedding Day'

Roses tolerant of partial shade or for north-facing walls

No rose will thrive and flower in dense shade but those listed below will perform well without direct sunlight. Roses suitable for training against walls are annotated (W).
Alba roses eg 'Alba Maxima', 'Alba Semiplena', 'Céleste', 'Félicité Parmentier'
'Albéric Barbier' (W)
'Andersonii'
'Complicata'
'Félicité Perpetué' (W)
'François Juranville' (W)
'Frühlingsgold'
'Gloire de Dijon' (W)
'Golden Showers' (W)
Hybrid Sweet Briars eg 'Manning's Blush'
'Madame Grégoire Staechelin' (W)
'Madame Plantier' (W)
'May Queen'
'Paulii'
'Splendens' (W)
'Veilchenblau' (W)
'Zéphirine Drouhin' (W)
'Zigeunerknabe'

Roses for ground cover

In large gardens, Climbing and Rambler roses can be allowed to grow in the open ground and will make large, weed-smothering mounds of growth. For smaller gardens, less vigorous varieties are needed which, although they are lax and mat-forming, will only cover one or two square metres of ground.

A few older varieties meet this criterion and there are many newly raised cultivars. Annual pruning is not usually necessary although it helps to rejuvenate the bushes by cutting them almost to the ground every few years. As with all ground cover, it is important to plant in soil that is completely free from perennial weeds such as couch grass or bindweed. These varieties are also extremely effective when planted to tumble over a retaining wall or the edge of a terrace.

'Daisy Hill'
'Dunwich Rose'
'Fairy Damsel'
'Fairyland'
'Fiona'
× *jacksonii* 'Max Graf'
'La Sevillana'
'Nozomi'
'Paulii'
'Pink Bells'
'Raubritter'
'Rosy Cushion'
'Scarlet Meidiland'
'Smarty'
'Swany'
'White Bells'

LOW-MAINTENANCE PLANTS
The following plants, once established, need the minimum attention if given suitable conditions and kept free of weeds. The shrubs should require virtually no pruning or other attention and are relatively free of disease.

The herbaceous plants do not require staking or regular division, are not invasive and are relatively free of disease and easy to grow.

Shrubs
Aucuba (7)
Berberis (3–8)
Buxus (6–8)
Cephalotaxus (6–7)
Chamaecyparis (3–9)
Cotoneaster (3–8)
Euonymus fortunei (5)
Fatsia (7)
Genista (5–9)
Griselinia (8)
Hamamelis (3–6)
Ilex (3–10)
Juniperus (3–9)
Leucothoë (5–9)
Mahonia (5–10)
Osmanthus (7–9)
Pachysandra (5)
Phillyrea (7–9)
Pieris (5–7)
Rhododendron (3–10)
Sarcococca (6–9)
Stephanandra (5–6)
Syringa (2–7)

Self-clinging climbers
Campsis radicans (5)
Decumaria (7–8)
Hedera (5–9)
Hydrangea anomala (5),
    H. petiolaris (5)
    and *H. serratifolia* (9)
Parthenocissus (3–9)
Pileostegia (9)
Schizophragma (5–7)
Trachelospermum (9)

Herbaceous and border plants
*Agapanthus**
Aruncus
*Bergenia**
Brunnera
Centaurea
Crambe
Dictamnus
Epimedium
Geranium (many)*
Hakonechloa
*Helleborus**
Hemerocallis
Hosta
Iris sibirica
*Liriope**
Pulmonaria
Rodgersia
Thalictrum

UNDERPLANTING
There is no need for herbaceous or mixed borders to look dull in spring: skilful underplanting of early flowers, which grow before deciduous shrubs or herbaceous plants come into leaf, will greatly extend the border's season of display. Spring flowers should be chosen so that they have finished growing before they are engulfed or cast into shade by the plants around them. Thus snowdrops can be planted with earlier-leafing plants than can *Geranium malviflorum*; however, this combines very well with hardy fuchsias which are cut to the ground each year by frost and come late into growth. Hostas are perhaps the perfect plants for this sort of association, all of them late enough into leaf to co-exist happily with snowdrops, anemones and celandines, while *H. plantaginea* is so tardy that it allows even more scope.

Anemone appenina, A. blanda,
    A. × *lipsiensis, A. nemorosa*
    and *A. ranunculoides*
Chionodoxa
Corydalis solida
    and *C. bulbosa*
Crocus
Eranthis
Erythronium
Galanthus
Geranium malviflorum
    and *G. tuberosum*
Hyacinthoides
Iris Reticulata cvs.
Muscari
Narcissus
Ranunculus ficaria
Scilla
Tulipa

Another sort of underplanting is the use of taller bulbs growing through a layer of lower plants. Suitable genera include lilies, camassias, galtonias and the taller alliums.

TENDER AND ANNUAL PLANTS
Whether for providing intense and continuous colour, bold – even tropical – foliage or simply for filling unforeseen gaps, tender and annual plants play a very important role in the garden and are worth a little extra work. They are also supremely useful for container planting, giving a strong focus of colour or form.

Agave
Argyranthemum
Calceolaria
Canna
Coleus
Cordyline
Cuphea
Dahlia
Eucalyptus
Fuchsia
Helichrysum
Heliotropium
Lantana
Melianthus
Nicotiana
Pelargonium
Penstemon
Petunia
Ricinus
Salvia
Verbena

COLOUR EFFECTS

Plant colours contribute to the atmosphere of a garden in all sorts of ways. The colours themselves have different qualities (green, for example, conjures a restful mood while red, its complementary, seems exciting), and how they are mixed or blended plays a vital part in the overall effect. In a group, some colours remain distinct while others blend together. Depending on the range of colours chosen and the way they are juxtaposed, the impression can be either lively or soothing. Whether you find a scheme cheerful or brash, subtle or dull, is partly a matter of taste, but to achieve the effects you want in your garden, you need to exploit the way colours interact naturally.

A detailed look at how individual colours influence one another demonstrates the technical meaning of some of the colour terms we commonly use, such as 'harmony' and 'contrast'.

The colour spectrum

We use the notion of the colour wheel, with segments depicting the six rainbow colours (red, orange, yellow, green, blue and violet) to define colour relationships. (The spectrum, of course, is a continuum, with many infinite gradations of green between yellow and blue, and so on.) Colours have other dimensions, too: they may be more or less intense, and they may darken towards black or pale towards white.

Examples based on spectral hues give a simplified picture, but nevertheless provide a useful guideline to the more complex interaction of colours in planting schemes.

Colours in context

The white background enhances the brightness of the drawings here, as if you had scattered a handful of leaves or petals on a page; garden colours, on the other hand, are inseparable from their usual green or earth-toned background, and from each other. Outdoors all sorts of other factors affect the colours we see. Among these is the general quality of the light – depending on climate, and on the time of day. The precise shape and texture of each flower or leaf will also influence how colour appears, revealing it clearly or as a diffuse impression.

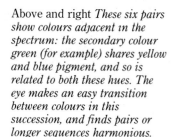

Above These three pairs of complementaries – opposites on the colour wheel – enhance one another by their extreme contrast. The eye finds nothing in common to link them, which exaggerates the difference. Using them together, especially at full intensity, makes vivid, 'colourful' pictures.

Above and right *These six pairs show colours adjacent in the spectrum: the secondary colour green (for example) shares yellow and blue pigment, and so is related to both these hues. The eye makes an easy transition between colours in this succession, and finds pairs or longer sequences harmonious.*

In two sets of related colours, lighter and darker values – like highlights and shadows – give the rather flat mixture dimension. A scheme based on 'hot' reds, oranges and yellows (far left) shines in bright sun, drawing the eye with its immediacy. A 'cooler' scheme (left) features blues, mauves and bluish-pinks – often in low intensities or pastel-pale tints, fading into white, or with slaty darker shades. Cloudy skies or shade enhance these subtleties. Shapes in this range become indistinct from afar, dissolving into the distance and increasing the sense of space.

Right *Harmonies of soft colours with silver foliage are a classic combination and, in large gardens, the whole spectrum can be used to plant harmonious borders on a grand scale. In smaller gardens, the colours should be restricted for best effect, as in this plan of pinks and mauves with purple and silver foliage.*

Many gardeners long for colour schemes with a little more 'bite'. Perhaps the most successful contrasting mix is of blue and yellow, both of which can seem rather flat on their own; together they make a piquant combination of complementary colours (below right).

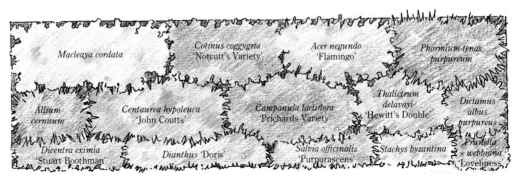

A border of colour harmonies

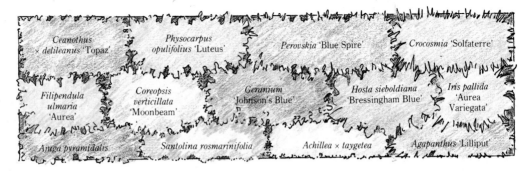

A border of colour contrasts

INDEX

Allee 28, 68, 124, 132
alcoves 40, 105
  mirror-backed 40, 49
'alpine meadow' 59
arbours 10, 62, 90, 124
  adding depth with 106
  as focal point 25
archways 17, 34, 40, 54, 67, 74, 112
  adding height with 54
  false 102, 104–5
  mirrored 40, 49, 104–5
  placing 30
  with focal point 25, 53
  with swing 53
architecture, elements of 12
asymmetrical gardens 31, 32, 44, 68, 121, 129
  diagonal axes 86, 87
aspect 12
  on checklist 8
avenues 124
aviary 56

Barbecues 66, 80, 129
  concealed 42
  planning 10
background/surroundings, limitations of 20
beds 90, 91
  central 90
  circular 55, 131
  with pool 87
  curved 47
  defining area with 88, 132
  raised 42, 44, 49, 55, 80, 94
    with steps 60, 71, 73
  recessed edges 55
  with shrub borders 97
  with 'windows' 83
beehives 10, 89
bird baths 10, 52
bog gardens 73, 86
borders: balanced by lawn 18, 51, 109
  breaks in 81
  contrasting/harmonizing 163
  defining area with 98
  dry shady 156
  dry sunny 154
  effect on length 128
  for enclosing areas 82, 132
  exposed 159
  'landscaped' 68–9
  moist shady 157
  moist sunny 155
  narrowing/widening 34, 68, 83, 115
  placing 137, 139
  planning 10, 14

and movement 18
  scale/proportion of 34
raised 42, 94
  on checklist 8
  low maintenance 57
  as screening 90, 129
  see also plantings
seaside 158–9
boulders 30, 47, 61
  artificial 123
boundaries 109, 124
  defining 27
  disguising 40, 47, 51, 68, 88, 92, 94, 102, 131
  distracting eye from 104, 106, 107
  fencing for 142
  integrating 40, 51
  measuring curved 136
  walls as 142
bricks/brickwork 20, 48–9, 58–9, 62–3, 68, 71, 80–1, 92, 109
  matching for continuity 32, 42, 53, 66, 80–1
  for paths/paving 15, 17, 48–9, 111, 108–9
  patterns 15, 17, 32, 48–9, 56–7, 73, 84–5
  visual effect of 22
  walls 140, 141
bridges 78, 86, 106, 118, 121

'**C**alm' areas 28
canals 87
  effect on length 95
checklist, of design elements 8–10, 11
  features to retain 134
  for drawing up plan 138
children see play areas
climate, prevailing 12
  see also shade, wind
clothes-drying areas 10
colour effects/themes 102, 104–5, 109, 162–3
  balance in 32
  'cold' 20
  in compartments 64
  complementary 162
  contrasting 163
  elements affecting choice 20
  in foliage 24
  of furniture 38
  harmonious 30, 31, 162–3
  'hot' 20, 163
    visual impact of 22
  monochrome themes 24
  pastel-hued 104
  and perspective 21

planning 150
  restricting 28, 32, 40, 163
  segregating 78
  use of competing 20
  on walls 53
compost heaps 10, 92
concealment/disguise, using 20
concrete 22, 94–5, 97
conifers: effects of pruning 34
  as focal points 24
containers/pots/urns 21, 30, 44, 45, 49, 59, 73, 109, 111, 147
  hanging 51
  with paving 10
  as focal points 15, 18, 21, 22
  planning 10
    balancing design with 32
  as screening 92
  see also planters
cottage garden 27, 62–3
country-house style 27
  miniature 51
courtyards 12, 40, 51, 129

Decking 30, 73, 86–7, 144
  with water garden 116
design, key when drafting 12
  restrictions/complications 12
  rules of thumb for 12
  principles: balance 32
    interest 36
    performance 38
    scale/proportion 34
    simplicity 28
    unity/harmony 30–1, 64, 78
'dining' room 64
distance, illusion of 20
double depth 112, 116
drainage, analysing 137
driveways 109, 110, 124, 126–7, 129, 130–1, 132
  on plan 138

Easy-access garden 83
elements: balancing space between 32
  judging appropriate size 34
  see also specific items
embankments 58
  with lawns 98
  planted 61, 85
  plotting levels for 137
  on sloping site 51
enclosed garden 12, 49
  choosing materials for 20
  see also garden 'rooms'
entertaining areas 10, 14, 38, 44, 76, 80

on checklist 8, 10
  see also family gardens; patios; terraces
evergreens 22, 24, 25, 78
  architectural use 24
  effect on balance 32
  fastigiate 22, 24

False perspective: creating 21
  on triangular site 92, 97
family garden 40, 44, 47, 51, 52–5, 66–9, 80–3, 94–7, 104–7, 116, 130–2
  effect of requirements on design 8, 10
fences 25, 40, 51, 62, 88–9, 108–9
  adding extra height 40
  around terrace 74
  choice of materials 20, 142–3
  defining spaces with 18, 78
  noting level changes 134, 137
  planning 142–3
    positioning for impact 22
    repeating patterns in 114
  as screening 124
    disguising boundaries 40, 46
    supplement to trees 11
  types 109, 143
  visual tricks with 102
  for winter viewing 76
flagstones 62
  in grass 19
flint 59
  walls 140, 141
focal points 21, 25, 26, 36, 42, 47, 57
  balancing 115
  beneath trees 60
  buildings as 25
  containers as 21
  framing 25, 54, 67
  effect of scaled-down 21
  ideal ornaments for 147
  illuminating, 148
  intermediate 69
  light-reflecting 76
  matching 64
  and movement 18
  multiple 106
  positioning 25
  outside the garden 25, 26
  placing in design 7
    cottage garden 62–3
    family garden 52
    front garden 102, 109, 110
    herb garden 49
    L-shaped sites 115–6, 118–9
    narrow sites 64, 66, 68–9, 71, 73, 76
    natural sites 89, 91
    rectangular sites 53, 80–1, 82, 84–5

roof garden 123
sloping sites 59, 71, 73
surrounding sites 127 8, 131, 132
triangular sites 94–5, 97, 98, 100
wide shallow sites 104–5, 106–7
secondary 84
'secret' 92
tall 55
terminal 74, 76, 87, 132
on walls 71, 85
see also individual items
formal garden 16, 17, 40, 42–5, 56–7, 63,
68–9, 73, 76, 77, 106, 114–6, 127,
129, 132
achieving balance in 32
in compartments 64
elliptic 51, 56–7
plans for 42
tree-lined entrance 124, 129
fountains 8, 12, 42, 147
as focal point 44
planning 10
plumbing for 12
wall-mounted 44, 53, 71, 84
see also ponds/pools
front garden 102, 108–11, 127
furniture 38, 112
permanent 44
roof garden 123
see also seating areas; seats

Garden 'rooms' 8, 12, 40, 64, 71, 73, 74,
76, 77, 78, 112, 124, 132
choosing materials for 20
connecting 44
with grass 78
dividing 51, 78
effect of shape on mood of 16
exploiting changes in level 78
organizing 40
as successive pictures 124
with swimming pool 128
garden surrounding the house 124–32
gates: mirror backed 105
wrought iron 105
gazebos: as 'balance' 32
in centre of lawn 131
shortening for false perspective 97
as focal point 25, 26
need on large site 124
raised 67
as seating area 47
grassy garden 132
gravel 22, 30, 57, 106
as alternative to grass 82
boulders in 47
brick edging to 110
as foil to plants 82
for paths 67, 73, 114
paving with 110
planting in 63, 110

in roof garden 123
self-binding 83, 98
greenhouses/glasshouses 64
automatic devices in 10
on checklist 8
as focal point 25
lean-to 53
screened off 131
ground cover: alternative to lawn 42, 74
considering when planning 10
effect on area shape 16
in front garden 102
low-maintenance 10
in paving joints 47
roses for 160–1
see also lawns; paths, paving
ground plans 16, 17
drawing up 12, 138
equipment for 134
indicating changes of level 134
final design 139
'reading' 14
realizing 152
see also plans

Handrails 51, 60, 71
hedges: as barriers 69
clipped 74
as focal point 26
visual impact of 22
curving 131
as dividers 67, 68–9, 74, 76, 115
driveway 127
flowering 131
lavender 27, 63
for privacy 132
front garden 109, 110
low: as bed edging 67, 68, 69, 102
around lawns 104
opening in 55
as screening 124, 129
for seaside sites 100
use of tall 17
as windbreaks 98
herb garden 48–9, 53
planning 10
horizontal elements: calculating scale/
position 12, 34
visual impact of 22

Informal gardens 10, 16, 46–7, 49, 68–9,
76, 83, 86–7, 107, 129
achieving balance in 32
in compartments 64
masking regular-shaped plot 40
planning 8
informality, on checklist 8

Kitchen garden 124
see also vegetable garden

Landmarks, as focal point 25
landscape: harmonizing materials to 30
planning transition to 30
landscape contractors, hiring 152
landscaping: 'hard' 140–6
'soft' 140, 150–1
lawn maintenance, considering when
planning 8
lawns 28, 56, 62, 68, 73, 90, 91, 98, 104–5,
112, 116, 121
alternatives to 10
as balance to planting 78
brick edging for 81
contoured 34, 81
broadening for visual effect 76, 80
shape determined by trees 73
'waisted' 78
on different levels 94–5, 97–8
lower level 94
pond in 131
raised 95, 107
echoing surrounding shapes 115
front garden 109, 129, 131, 132
future use for 10
linking separate areas with 116
as play areas 68, 94, 104, 132
positioning on plan 129, 138
right proportions for 34
shade tolerant 42
'swirling' 131
visual effect of 22
leaf size, as design element 24
levels changes: creating two 51
with decking 86
effect on viewpoint 14
on triangular site 92
see also lawns, sloping gardens
lighting: to illuminate sculpture 74
planning 148, 149
low maintenance garden 44, 54–5, 57, 63,
82, 97, 100
planning 10
plants 161

Maintenance, on checklist 8
meadow garden 88, 91, 119, 127
mirrors: for extra depth 40, 49, 68, 102,
105
Moorish garden 87
movement, creating 18, 19, 34, 36 passim
mowing, designing for easier 10
mystery, creating sense of 36

Natural garden 88–91
new gardens, sequence of building
operations 152

niches 56
with focal point 25
fountain in 59
noise, providing protection from 11
nursery catalogues, selecting from 34

Obelisks, planted 69
open garden 69
orchard, screened off 131
orientation/aspect, checking when
planning 137
ornaments 10, 25
for balance 104
as focal points 25, 31, 36
harmonizing with surroundings 31
planning 147–9
see also containers/pots/urns; statues,
etc.

Parapets 51, 60
parking areas 124
surfaces for 109
parterre 102, 132
passageways 18, 34
paths 16, 17, 18, 19, 32, 47, 49, 67, 68, 69,
72, 74, 76, 83, 88, 94, 95, 98, 100,
102, 104, 114, 115
as 'backbone' of design 66, 76, 124
changing direction of 55, 68, 74
creating movement with 17, 19, 69
curving 76
focal point in 62
for depth 53
for wheelchairs 83
decking 116
easy-access 83
front garden 108–9, 110, 111
grass 86, 88, 91, 107, 118–9, 131
to focal point 26
around 49
illuminating 148
incorporated in terrace 98
interrupted 77
linking elements with 78, 80–1, 126
linking two levels 59
material: bark-chip 83, 121
brick 16, 115
changes in 67, 82
flint 59
gravel 49, 116
natural stone 88
paving 19
peat 83
random surfaces 56
single type throughout 51, 64, 78
visual effect of 17, 22
narrowing 21, 34, 92, 97
as passageways 34
placing in design 7
for harmony 30

planning considerations 14
unifying element 124
serpentine 116
softening lines of 51
through archways 53, 54
as cycle track 55
water running under 87
winding 78
'woodland' 28
see also walkways
patios: enclosed 73
natural stone 83
positioning 135, 138
see also seating areas and terraces
paving 10, 15, 28, 42, 47, 62–3, 64, 92, 100, 102, 144–5
as alternative to grass 38
changing direction of 44
driveway 109
effect of too much 34
front garden 102
interplanted 44, 47, 49, 62, 121
with planting holes 76
low maintenance 44
materials 20, 144–5
choosing for harmony 30
natural stone 60, 71, 76, 80, 104, 144–5
same type throughout 53, 66, 94
see also individual items
pale-coloured 59, 106
planning 144–5
randomly laid 49
right proportions for 34
roof garden 123
staggering joints in 69
surrounding house 127
visual effect of texture/pattern 16, 22
varying width/shapes in 64
visually enlarging area with 40, 59
pavilions 56, 115
as focal point 49
with tennis court 126–7
pebbles: visual effect of 22
as path edging 98
pergolas 34, 63, 70–1, 87, 98–9, 100, 101, 112, 122–3, 148
dividing areas with 78, 124
for extra depth 40, 44
as focal point 147
as frame 87, 132
planning 148
for shade 131
visual impact of 22
effect of reducing height 21
perspective: creating illusions of 102
effect of colours on 20
effect on design elements 14
to enlarge space 28
when drawing plan 139
see also false perspective
pillars/poles, rope swagged 27, 132

pine bark granules 55
see also paths
planning: measuring plot for 134
time factor in 30, 32
plans: L-shaped garden 112–23
large rectangular 78–91
long narrow 64–77
looking ahead 10–11
making 133–52
making checklist for 8, 10
modifying 38
reading a plan 14
small rectangular 51–63
small square 40–9
in three dimensions 14–15
triangular 92–101
very narrow 74–7
wide shallow 102–11
plant hardiness 154
planters 42, 49, 63, 74, 87
matching throughout garden 69, 74, 76, 97
roof garden 122–3
softening effect with 81
plantings 36, 55, 59, 62, 63, 71, 78, 86, 88, 90, 92, 95, 98, 102, 104, 106, 109, 110, 111, 118, 121, 123
balance in 32
bold-leaved 86
behind open steps 73
seen through frame 54
concealed lighting in 148
with gravel 47
measuring 136
perfectly proportioned 34
scented 94
repeating for unity 78
restricted plant types 114
one type only 97, 106, 109
as screening 21, 36, 88, 119, 124, 127, 128
disguising boundaries 47, 124
separating themes/areas with 78
to soften effect 71, 77
symmetrical 16, 84
varying height in 68–9
year-round interest 47
plants: climbing: adding depth with 49
for dry shade 156
for dry sun 155
for moist shade 157
for moist sun 155
as screens 10, 20, 40
for seaside areas 157–8
softening hard surfaces 10
for total shade 155–6
for exposed sites 158–9
as focal points 25
foliage 45
herbaceous: for dry shade 156
for dry sun 155
for moist shade 157

for moist sun 155
for total shade 156
for Japanese theme 30
low maintenance 161
perfumed 38
planning type/quantity 150, 153–61
rules for grouping 32
structural role of 12, 24
soil suitability for 30, 137
tender/annuals 161
and visual impact 24
water/bog garden 159
plantsman's garden 8, 44, 55
plaques 85, 147
play areas 7, 8, 12, 44, 53, 55, 64, 67, 68, 69, 76, 90, 104, 106, 112, 114, 116, 126, 129
future use for 10
planning layout 139
separate 53, 55
surfaces for 10, 55
playhouse 98
ponds/pools 10, 12, 32, 42, 44, 45, 46, 66, 78, 84–7, 89, 91, 114–7, 118, 131, 132
against wall 68
on checklist 8
dangers of 10
as focal point 81, 100
with fountain 59, 63, 74, 76, 95, 123
in a grotto 60
incorporating border 83
as linking element 112
Moorish-style 78, 87
plumbing for 12
raised 44, 45, 53
reflected light from 47
screened 107
potagers 10
'practical' garden 63
privacy 40, 47, 49, 62
for swimming pool 129

Retaining walls 60, 142
inter-planted 60
plotting levels for 137
seating incorporated in 66
on sloping site 51
viewpoint and 14
rock garden 60, 61, 72, 98
rond-point 64
roof garden 112, 122–3
roses, choosing 160–1
tunnel of 85
rustic work 62

Screens 15, 36, 123, 124
planning 10
types 55, 60, 90
principle of 15
as space dividers 44, 129, 131

for swimming pool 90
visual impact of 24
see also fences; shrubs; trees
sculpture 12, 36, 47, 112
garden for displaying 74
see also statues
seaside garden 98–100
plants for 157–9
seating areas 38, 63, 76, 88, 90, 94
checking orientation 137
on decking 86
enclosed 3, 68
placing 8, 10, 16, 36, 42, 47, 49, 53, 55, 59, 60, 63, 64, 66, 68, 71, 73, 76, 78, 88, 104, 106, 127, 132, 138, 139
hidden 90
light/shade and 11
terrace as 57, 74, 84
under trees 60, 68, 69, 76
as vantage point 100
seats 8
for balance 32
choosing 75
dual-purpose 40, 42, 123
as focal point 25, 26, 44, 69, 75, 115, 131, 132, 147
hidden 36, 76
low walls as 94
multiple 56, 57, 59, 69, 87, 131
placing 40, 44, 56, 62, 64, 68, 69, 76, 88, 94, 124
under trees 90, 107, 121, 131
water running under 87
secret garden 36, 64, 74, 112
setts 42, 47, 62, 72, 74, 109
in steps 61
shade 40, 160
effect on design 11, 137
focal point in 42
plants for 155–7
problems with 40
reflected light in 47
roses for 160
'shadow lines' 22, 24
shadows: checking fall of 137
shredded bark 22
sheds 10, 64, 92
decorative 114
screened 20, 107
shrubs 45, 55, 76
calculating size of 34
choosing: for dry shade 156
for dry sun 154
for exposed site 158–9
low maintenance 161
for moist shade 157
for moist sun 155
for seaside areas 157–8
for total shade 155–6
for water/bog garden 159
clipped 57, 74, 105, 106
planning positions 139, 150

THE
GARDEN PLANNER

THE
GARDEN PLANNER

ROBIN WILLIAMS

FRANCES LINCOLN

For Ann

Frances Lincoln Limited,
Apollo Works, 5 Charlton Kings Road,
London NW5 2SB

The Garden Planner
© Frances Lincoln Limited 1990
Text and illustrations © Robin Williams 1990

All rights reserved
No part of this publication may be reproduced, stored in a retrieval system,
or transmitted, in any form, or by any means, electronic, mechanical, photocopying,
recording or otherwise without prior permission of the publishers.

British Library Cataloguing in Publication Data
Williams, Robin
The garden planner.
1. Gardens. Planning
I. Title
712'.6
ISBN 0-7112-0605-8

Printed and bound in Hong Kong by Kwong Fat Offset Printing Co. Ltd
Set in Century Old Style by Ace Filmsetting Ltd, Frome, Somerset
Originated in Hong Kong by Evergreen Colour Separation Co. Ltd
First Frances Lincoln Edition: February 1990

3 5 7 9 8 6 4

CONTENTS

Introduction 6

GARDEN DESIGN 7
Elements of Design 12
Design Principles 27

GARDEN PLANS 39
Small Square Gardens 40
Small Rectangular Gardens 50
Long Narrow Gardens 64
Large Rectangular Gardens 78
Triangular Gardens 92
Wide Shallow Gardens 102
L-Shaped Gardens 112
Gardens Surrounding the House 124

MAKING THE PLAN 133

PLANNING FOR PLANTS 153

Index 164
Useful Addresses 167
Acknowledgments 168

INTRODUCTION

Many people would like to be able to plan their own gardens, but to the uninitiated garden design can often seem highly complex and theoretical. In this book I want to remove the mystique that surrounds the subject, and show how accessible it can be.

The first chapter, *Garden Design*, shows how to start at the very beginning – thinking about what you want from your own garden. It then explains the elements of garden design – how to give structure to a garden and how different elements and differently shaped areas create atmosphere, style, movement and repose.

Next, *Garden Plans* offers a wealth of different garden designs as a source both of inspiration and practical help. It provides plans for different shapes and sizes of plot, illustrating and describing the main designs in great detail, with perspective drawings showing how the flat plan looks in three-dimensions, and giving many alternative examples. This section can be used in various ways. One course of action is to select the garden outline that most resembles your own and see at a glance a clutch of off-the-peg layouts that make the most of that shape. The best approach, however, if you want to gain the most from the wealth of designs displayed, is to browse through the illustrations, as if wandering through real gardens. This is always the ideal way of finding inspiration as well as ideas that translate from one situation to another. If a feature or shape catches your eye, read the explanatory text to see why it has been chosen, how it relates to the overall shape and style of the plot, and then apply this principle to your own garden to gauge whether it will work in that context, or how it might be adapted. Studying the designs and perspective realizations is also of great practical help, enabling you to clarify the relationship between a plan and what it will look like in three dimensions. The process should also help you see your plot in design terms, and allow you to work out your own original planning ideas more effectively.

Making the Plan brings all the practical considerations together and shows, step-by-step, how to make your plan. This starts with measuring the site and drawing it accurately, analysing the plot and making a functional plan of what is possible within it, and drawing up an outline design. The design is then filled with practical details of plants and man-made structures such as walls, fences, paths and steps, and the plan completed by getting the work done and in the right order.

Finally, *Planning for Plants* helps you to choose the plants that will best fill your designs and to decide how to use them, offering lists of plants that work well in particular situations, and explaining how to plant for the best colour effects.

As a professional designer, I can think of nothing more satisfying than taking on a garden and designing it – except perhaps the special rewards, given to those who design their own gardens, of watching it develop and mature according to plan, so becoming a three-dimensional, ever-changing living picture. I hope this book brings these pleasures within everyone's reach.

GARDEN DESIGN

When you start to think about designing your own garden there are two main considerations. Firstly you need an understanding of what you want in and from your garden. This involves making a list of what to include in it (terraces, grass, fountains, roses) and thinking about who will use it and for what purposes (children for play, adults for relaxation).

Secondly you need an understanding of the design process – how the three-dimensional structure of a garden is created from a flat plan. The placing of elements – trees, paths, focal points – within a garden forms structural shapes: the shapes themselves create movement or repose, and the elements have their own visual impact on the garden atmosphere.

Garden designs must fit their context, suiting the house and what already exists on the site. They should also exhibit the qualities, such as simplicity and harmony, that form the basis of a good design.

STARTING POINTS

The design process begins with two distinct starting points: the actuality of the site, and your ideas and ideals about a garden. The details of the plan you evolve should be a happy resolution between these. A detailed analysis of the site will answer the questions of what is feasible, and of how – and how many of – your objectives, perhaps apparently incompatible ones, can be achieved. But first you have to have an idea of what those objectives are.

A sense of purpose
What sort of garden are you aiming to create? What do you want in it and how are you going to use it? The best way to answer these questions is by making a checklist of everything you want from a garden. The list will probably be a mixture that includes: objects, such as a pond or a greenhouse; activities, such as sunbathing or entertaining; desirable

qualities, such as informality, ease of maintenance or an open aspect; and notes about you or your family's needs and preferences, such as a safe play space for toddlers or raised beds that will be easy on your bad back.

To start with you should think about the role the garden is going to play. Questions to consider are, for example, whether you want to use it primarily for relaxation, and if so will this include playing games as well as just sitting enjoying the view? Or are you such a keen plantsperson that you would rather devote most of your time to cultivation?

The design of any garden should be broadly influenced by who is to use it, and when. The requirements of a family with young children are not the same as those of a professional couple, or of retired or disabled people. Some plots are actively gardened by enthusiasts; others are simply regarded as an outdoor living space, a useful extension of the house in which plants may happen to grow. Some gardens are used only at weekends. Some come to life in the evenings. Some are neglected in the summer, when the owners go away on holiday for several weeks at a time.

People also have different priorities. Some don't mind an informal muddle, others like things to be meticulously neat. People also vary considerably not only in how much time they have available, but also in their attitude to their gardening time: what is a chore to one is a pleasurable or therapeutic activity to another. Both weeding and lawn maintenance come into this class of activity.

When you are thinking about these issues in relation to your own garden, be realistic both about the amount of upkeep that you are prepared to expend on it, and about whether the potential features that you specify on your detailed checklist are really compatible with the way you

Left *In this garden, planned as a quiet oasis in which to relax, plants are used as the green furnishings in a garden room. Handsome man-made elements, like the bench and fountain, are of equal importance.*

Right *In a plantsman's garden, you need to give priority to providing the conditions in which favourite plants will thrive. In high summer the layout of this design is almost eclipsed by the exuberant flowers.*

want to use the garden. If your family enjoys vigorous ball games, beautiful but fragile plants edging your herbaceous borders won't survive; if very young children use the garden often, a natural pond will be too dangerous; if you don't enjoy the regular mowing or careful maintenance a lawn needs, it might be better to choose some other form of ground cover.

Once you have thought about these general ideas, you can compile a more detailed checklist and see how well these specific ideas will fit in with the purposes you have considered. The items on the checklist might include favourite plants or plant themes, ornaments, areas for sitting, sunbathing, cooking out, and practicalities such as climbing frames and compost heaps. Now is the time to list the garden delights you always wanted – a fountain perhaps, or a rose arbour, a birdbath, a barbecue, a beehive.... The next stage will be to try to plan them into the plot.

Some of these specific requirements may be completely in line with the general ideas. Others may need more thought to make them fit in comfortably, or special designs so they work in the context of your garden – especially where space is at a premium. For example an area may have to serve more than one purpose. You can accommodate useful and edible plants attractively in a primarily ornamental garden – herb beds and potagers, pots, and climbing beans or peas as vertical features or screens are all attractive. You can incorporate low-maintenance strategies to make mowing easier or to suppress weeds, and automatic devices can reduce the amount of attention something like a greenhouse needs. Functional utilities such as compost heaps, mower-sheds or clothes-drying areas, can often be made attractive, disguised and camouflaged, or screened away out of sight. Fitting these ideas and practicalities together is all part of a good design.

Looking ahead

In practice, a good design will look ahead. You would like a water feature, so you should plan a layout with a safe sandpit or play area or lawn that will later become a pool when the children are older. You would like a herbaceous border against a sunny wall but can't devote enough time to it yet, so for the time being you could plant low-maintenance ground cover or lawn. You plan a shrubbery or 'wild' area until you have the time and money to build a summerhouse.

Left *A paved area beside the house provides a convenient place to sit and relax or take meals, and provides children with an alternative play area when the lawn is wet. Containers and climbing plants soften the hard surfaces of paving and house.*

Right *An informal area on the outer fringes of a garden is a lure for wildlife, with a pool making it doubly attractive. A margin of longer grass bridges the transition between a not-too-closely mown lawn and a backdrop of trees. Although a wild garden, once established, needs relatively little maintenance, periodic intervention by the gardener is vital to prevent the unacceptable face of nature from taking over.*

Don't rush things at any stage. It is a good idea to allow plenty of time for quietly gathering your thoughts about the project as a whole, and making sure that you come up with as comprehensive a statement of requirements as possible. You need time to mull over the list of your ideas and needs.

Time is also useful in getting to know what the site has to offer. An established garden – even one whose design you dislike – can contain all sorts of hidden treasures. Horticultural gems may lurk under the soil waiting for the appropriate time of year to show themselves, or a rather dull plant will suddenly transform itself into a glorious mass of flowers or autumn colour. A wait-and-see policy is recommended where there might very well be something worth saving.

But delay is also valuable for getting to know *any* site, even a bare one. You have to live in a house before you really know its advantages and disadvantages, and in the same way, only time will reveal the full potential that a site has to offer. Changing weather conditions might make you realize that you need to provide shelter from wind or noise coming from a particular quarter. New seasons can present radical differences in the amounts of sunshine or shade in particular corners of the garden, and this will certainly be taken into account when you plan the siting of any seating area, and influences the choice of plants too. Deciduous trees seen in winter without their foliage may suddenly seem inadequate as a screen, making you decide to plan to replace them with evergreens or supplement them with a fence; on the other hand, you might find you like the extra light better than the leafy summer canopy, and after due deliberation decide to do away with them.

ELEMENTS OF DESIGN

Garden design is an art form. Like all good design, its aim is to create a satisfying composition. This must please the senses – especially the sense of sight. It must also be functional, fulfilling the designer's brief and fitting the user's intended purpose. Successful design looks good *and* works.

The art of garden design is particularly affected by restrictions and complications. In the first place, a garden relates to its associated architecture and its surroundings. The relationship may be a very close one: in some of the great historic gardens, plants grow between walls and steps that match those of the house. On a smaller scale, this relationship occurs in a modern design where patio doors opening on to terraces or courtyards bring the garden indoors. Occasionally a garden is separate or remote from a house; sometimes it is completely enclosed so that the outside world does not impinge. However, in some respects a garden always remains *part* of the surrounding landscape. Shelter, drainage, irrigation, soil quality and so on can be improved more or less, but the garden's aspect (whether it gets morning sun, for example) and the prevailing climate (high rainfall, mild winters, and so on) are factors that you cannot alter.

Secondly, garden design brings together elements from a number of different disciplines. Architecture and horticulture play the major parts, but there may be supporting roles for carpentry, stone masonry, sculpture and so on, or perhaps plumbing where ponds and fountains may involve complicated hydraulic engineering, and perhaps even psychology where, for example, a designer needs to contrive a plan that will keep ball games and bicycles off prized planting schemes.

Thirdly, all the personal tastes, whims and prejudices of the owners and the practical requirements of the users have to be fed into the design process.

To create a harmonious whole in these complex circumstances, there are a number of more or less practical tools of the trade and some useful rules of thumb. The garden designer draws on building technology for practical techniques and on art and architecture for general aesthetic principles (the six key ones are discussed towards the end of this chapter). The materials used to realize the design are at least in part growing, living plants, constantly changing, and so horticultural considerations are needed to choose the right plants and to keep them healthy and so looking good. But the plants' part in the scheme of things is structural, just like that of the man-made elements, and providing a sound underlying structure is at the heart of good garden planning.

Of course, to design a beautiful garden you do not need to master the whole range of disciplines involved – you can employ the expertise of others. However, you do need to be aware of the elements of garden design, and to understand the guiding principles and how they work in practice.

From the checklist described earlier, and the site specifications that are dealt with in *Making the Plan*, you can begin sketching out ideas and design solutions for a given site. This chapter now looks at what is involved in this process. First may come some projected design shapes to make a good strong ground plan, taking into account the shape and size of the plot. Next this layout is realized in terms of the appropriate hard and soft ingredients – building materials and plants.

The key to the design at this stage of drafting plans on paper – in two dimensions – is never to lose sight of the fact that you are always working in three dimensions, and that time will add a fourth.

Good garden architecture encompasses both man-made structures and plant forms. In this well-designed garden, the 'hard' elements of pond, pergola and stone ornaments are matched by a range of plants chosen for their individual leaf shape or their overall habit to contribute to a bold, balanced picture.

PLANNING IN THREE DIMENSIONS

The elements from which a garden is composed consist of spaces and shapes. Using metaphors drawn from painting, you can think of the blank (or, in the case of existing gardens, not-so-blank) canvas on which the composition is conceived as the overall area of the plot. The colours on the artist's palette are plants and man-made structures. These have mass, and define the spaces, shapes and areas within the design.

It is important to practise 'translating' the flat ideas you see in plans on paper into three-dimensional images existing in the garden space. You need to visualize how big the rounded outline representing a tree will be in reality – not only scaled up to a full-size circle on the ground, but also as a towering mass overhead – and where its shadow will pass during the day. You will need to think in practical terms – perhaps by physically pacing such areas – about how wide to make a path that will take a wheelbarrow or two people walking side-by-side, or (just as in kitchen design) how much space to allocate around, say, a sitting or barbecue area.

Any geometrical figures or curvy lines that look fine on paper must look equally good from the ground. The shapes of beds and borders are sometimes pleasing in themselves but contribute nothing to the overall scene. They may be out of proportion to the size of the garden, or the lines and forms of the design may be 'wrong' – confusing the eye or creating an imbalance. It is important to remember that whatever the shape of a space or area, it will close up or foreshorten in perspective when viewed from a normal standing position. What starts out as a circle on the plan will appear elliptical on the ground; a rectangle may appear square. A grassed area with an outline of curves on the plan may appear as a series of acute and pointless zigzags in the real lawn. You can gain a good idea of how shapes on paper will actually appear by looking down the plan in a particular direction while holding the edge up near eye level.

Real gardens offer even more changes of viewpoint. What you see of a flat plot varies depending on whether you are

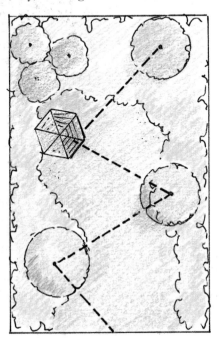

Left It is useful to develop the knack of 'reading' a plan and visualizing it in three dimensions. On the plan, the dotted lines show that the vertical elements are fairly evenly spaced along similar angles. The sketch shows how the elements close up in perspective, and how the tree in the foreground partially conceals the summerhouse, adding interest.

Right A garden in which abrupt changes of level occur offers very different views from either end. Seen from above, the lower terraces almost disappear down a slope, whereas from the lowest viewpoint the retaining walls assume far greater impact than the horizontal surfaces.

Good designs work well on several levels. Glimpsed from a distance, a container planted with Lychnis coronaria, *set in a pool of sunlight and framed by a soft fringe of planting, makes an attractive low focal point. As you approach closer, along the path whose lines are partly disguised by the lush planting of* Alchemilla mollis, *the container is revealed to be the centrepiece of a circular paving pattern of brickwork, which is echoed in the surrounding walls and a curved stone bench. The full effect of this motif of concentric circles is best appreciated when seen from a height, but it also makes a balanced picture from other parts of the garden.*

sitting or standing on the terrace, or looking down from the ground-floor or upper-storey windows in the house. Some of the formal plans in the next chapter, while satisfying at ground level, are especially rewarding to look down on from the house. With a sloping garden the differences become more extreme. When dramatic changes of level occur along the length of a garden, two quite different gardens can appear: depending on where the viewer is standing, there will be either a series of diminishing plateaux or a series of embankments or retaining walls, one on top of the other.

Moving around within a garden creates a lot of different pictures, too. On the plan you need to work out what will be seen from where, and what will be screened. However small the area, there can be some corner hidden away behind a curtain of planting that draws the visitor in to investigate, and so to find and enjoy a new viewpoint. The principle of the screen in all its forms is invaluable in garden planning. By separating features or areas of interest you enable each to make a composition in its own right.

THE GROUND PLAN

For the different parts of the garden to hang together to make a satisfying picture, a cohesive structure is needed. This can be formal, informal or gradations in between according to taste, but it needs to fit the overall shape and layout of the garden; symmetry, for example, needs a regular and level site, and symmetrical planting can call for a fair amount of maintenance to keep it in shape. The structure can, if desired, be obvious; for example, a formal layout could be complex and intended to be appreciated as a pattern in itself. For an informal garden, the underlying framework may be almost entirely disguised by planting so that the garden looks as if it has grown up naturally, but some structure needs to exist in order that the whole functions as an enjoyable garden instead of lapsing into uncontrollable wilderness.

Whether they are laid out in terms of formal geometric figures or more loosely defined, differently shaped areas on the ground influence the mood of a garden. Some shapes are decidedly static, the most restful area being one of equal pro-portions, such as a circle, hexagon or square. Within such areas there is no incentive to go anywhere, so they make excellent seating areas or places to pause and relax. A long, narrow space on the other hand acts like a corridor, encouraging movement – a path is the ultimate example. In between these extremes, generously proportioned rectangular and oval spaces create a calm but not too static atmosphere in which relaxed meandering seems natural.

The designs in the next chapter show examples of these shapes in a whole range of different types of garden. They also demonstrate how detailing within such areas – especially in the ground covering, such as the pattern in which paving is laid – can emphasize the effect of the basic shape, reinforcing a static mood or using directional lines to suggest movement.

One vital design point is that these shapes should never be arbitrary – the design should define them appropriately. If a path curves, it should curve around some object, such as a tree or a man-made vertical element.

Right *A formal ground plan makes good use of a regular rectangular plot that is virtually flat – it rises in a series of wide platforms and the steps are an integral part of the design, adding to its interest. The wide expanses of brick paving suggest a leisurely tour of the garden; near the seats at either end of the cross-axis the linear pattern changes to radiating semicircles, signalling a place to pause. The cool symmetry of the plan on paper is softened when it is realized in terms of plants. Standard trees, tall hedges, an arch and a summerhouse are all vertical elements that break the rectangle into more intimate areas. Changing patterns of light and shadow create their own new patterns throughout the day.*

Left *Whether the overall layout is formal or informal, the details of the planting and materials in which the plan is interpreted influence the garden atmosphere enormously, reinforcing the sense of structure or blurring it considerably. A path by definition suggests movement, but its character will have an effect on the quality of the journey. Herring-bone bricks (left) convey you briskly from A to B, but in a decorative, traditional spirit. The 'homespun' texture of a patterned path of loose bricks and stone (centre) and its strong horizontal line, suggest a more measured pace. And a mown path (right), winding through an area of long grass keeps the leisurely, informal feel of a natural garden.*

MOVEMENT WITHIN THE GARDEN

Different shaped areas in a garden not only create different moods, they also promote movement from one space to another. There are various ways of defining such spaces; even within the smallest garden much can be done to impart character through the use of just a few vertical elements – suggested areas are just as valuable as specific ones. Space permitting, however, the most successful way to create areas is by making the surrounds – be they plants, walls or fences – high enough so that they may not be seen over. The optimum is at least eye-level, but the size of the area must always be considered since high levels in a small space will naturally emphasize the limited area. When designing a garden it is also always necessary to bear in mind its use and, if an area is to be used mainly for sitting in, then eye-level height from a sitting position is perfectly adequate for the surroundings.

The more an area is elongated, either as a rectangle or elipse, the more a sense of directional movement increases and can be used to advantage, suggesting anything from a leisurely stroll to a hurried walk. The psychology behind this principle is well worth exploring and should be employed according to the demands of the area. For example, a herbaceous border is not something to pass by without pausing to enjoy the colours and textures of plants and their relationships with each other. Such a border should be placed where the tempo is leisurely and slow. A broadly rectangular or elliptically shaped space would provide such an atmosphere – a border is best associated with a broad path or lawn.

Movement increases as the dimensions become more disproportionate until ultimately a narrow passageway results. The higher the sides or surrounds, the narrower and longer the area will appear. Again, spaces like these have their uses, making valuable links between the more open parts of the garden. They provide a sense of suspense and if they curve so that the next area is unseen, they can add a strong element of surprise. Narrow walkways can be used to theatrical effect as, historically, they often were. In gardens grand enough to afford the space they could be blind at one end, with a terminal focal point consisting of a vase or statue.

Right: *The diamond-shaped flagstones set in mown grass give this vista a strong and purposeful direction. The high, dense planting on the left increases the sense of movement while the lower plants and openings on the right promise new areas to explore. High planting on both sides could easily engulf the space, suggesting such a fast walk along the avenue that the plants would not be fully enjoyed.*

Left: *These two paths are exactly the same length and width but, by altering the treatment of the sides, the sense of movement, and consequently the mood, is vastly different. On the right, the planting is close to the path, immediately offering an incentive to move along it faster than with the path on the left. Obviously, the higher the adjacent planting the narrower the path will seem and so movement will hasten. Conversely, the path on the left suggests a leisurely stroll, for the planting is set well back, providing room on each side of the path, offering breathing space and a less hurried sense of direction.*

GARDEN COMPOSITIONS IN CONTEXT

Comparatively little gardening offers absolute freedom of choice to compose with the materials on your palette as you will. Occasionally in a completely enclosed garden or separate garden compartment you can do something different without a clash of styles, just as you can decide what colour scheme and what kind of plant to put in a particular island bed or an individual container.

More often what is visible in the background or surroundings creates the context and limits your scope in some way. What colours you choose to plant in a particular bed may be influenced by the tone of the wall or fence behind it, or the presence of some existing plant in a particular colour, which perhaps provides the keynote to a whole scheme. Sometimes some other factor in the equation influences the choice. It may be, for example, that you want to exploit the perspective effects of colour values. Vibrant, 'hot' colours like red and yellow tend to stand out and give the impression of nearness while the 'cooler' greys and blues, tend to seem further away. So, perhaps you will decide to create the illusion of distance by using misty-toned plants.

This need to see design ideas in context is just as true with the 'hard' garden elements. Paving or fencing materials, for example, that are radically different from those in which the house is built – or indeed from each other – need to be

very carefully vetted to prevent a clash of styles. Even one category, such as bricks, can make a disruptive picture when different kinds, new and old, and varying colour tones are thoughtlessly mixed. In general, because of the multitude of individual elements – different plants, objects, surfaces, surrounds – that make up even the smallest garden, it is better to opt for as few competing styles and tones as possible.

Looked at positively, what seems like a limitation often provides a useful starting point for creating an interesting and harmonious scheme. It is also a creative challenge to work within the limits of a garden plot, using planning and planting ingenuity to improve on what exists and to overcome problems. You might have to call on the compositional elements of climbing plants or trellis to cover up an unsightly wall or shed. You can plan the position of trees, shrubs or man-made screens to disguise eyesores on the boundary, in or outside the garden. A skilful arrangement will focus attention on some interesting feature and away from something less attractive. If the elements are chosen well and positioned artfully, no one need realize their initial purpose as concealment or disguise.

Assess the visual impact of the garden framework – the house, boundaries, existing features that you wish to keep – and then judge what kind of compositions will be appropriate.

Right *So understated are the visual effects in this garden picture that you are hardly aware that your gaze is being gently manipulated. The axial view across the lawn is softened and blurred by planting that disguises its geometry. Nevertheless the eye is drawn to a focal point – an urn on a pedestal discernible in the shade beneath a deep hood of foliage. This and its surrounding plant interest holds the attention so firmly that it is possible to disregard the buildings in evidence beyond the garden boundary.*

Left *A degree of false perspective can be introduced by making elements physically smaller or shorter as they recede from a particular viewpoint. The spacing of vertical elements and their relative heights can shorten or lengthen a garden visually. These two garden layouts are the same size overall, but the one on the right is carefully contrived to appear more spacious. Towards the far end the path actually narrows, the trees are pruned smaller, and the pergola reduces in height. A scaled-down focal point helps give the illusion of distance, and the use of misty grey-blue planting as a backdrop makes this part of the picture seem to dissolve and recede; an eye-catching yellow or red tone here would make the vanishing point seem a good deal closer.*

VISUAL IMPACT

Garden structure consists of areas, shaped and defined by the vertical elements that surround and intrude on them. What these areas and elements are like, and the way they are used, creates the atmosphere of the garden.

Each different surface – hard or soft – has its own visual impact. This can be strong, drawing the attention as does the solid, dark outline of a columnar evergreen or a contrasting mass of coloured foliage or flowers, especially yellows and reds, which stand out clearly and which the eye can 'read' at a distance. Other vertical elements are more subtly shaped and textured; the amorphous mid-green leaves of many deciduous trees and plants are not by themselves eye-catching. Some vertical elements – particularly man-made ones – are textured with 'shadow lines' running in a particular direction (usually horizontally or vertically), which affects their role in the garden. The vertical shadow lines of a picket fence emphasize its height; the continuous horizontal lines of the mortar in a brick wall carry the eye along its length. A clipped hedge makes a smooth, continuous texture, but a closely planted line of fastigiate conifers creates a clear rhythm of verticals.

Horizontal elements – especially the flat surfaces such as lawns, paving and paths – may also be more or less smooth, textured or patterned and they, too, affect the mood of the garden or at least the area they cover. Surfaces that are smooth, regular or neat set an atmosphere of formality; rough irregular or overgrown ones bring an air of informality. Grass, gravel, shredded bark, paving, pebbles, brick, concrete – all create textures as various as the different floor coverings that can be used indoors. Geometrical, linear patterning such as that in paving (or even neat mowing stripes) contributes additional, usually formal, character as well as influencing or emphasizing shape and direction.

The aim of composition, in a garden as anywhere, is to

Below *While some degree of contrast creates interesting tensions in any composition, too much causes conflict, resulting in a restless, unsatisfying picture. The tall, solid-looking shapes of columnar evergreens make such emphatic verticals that they need to be carefully positioned. The vertical shadow lines of the fence (left) set up a steady rhythm that harmonizes with the evergreens; against the predominantly horizontal pattern lines of the wall (right), they strike a more jarring note.*

Right *Beyond the enclosed area defined by a pergola, an open space fringed by less formal planting beckons invitingly, with an urn dramatically framed at its far end. The pergola is made of poles rather than sawn timber, and its design is not tightly symmetrical, giving it a rustic quality well in keeping with the woodland atmosphere; it almost seems to be growing, like the wisteria and Virginia creeper stems that entwine it. The dense foliage of box at the pergola's base anchors the structure.*

A good foliage composition in a border provides long-term plant 'furnishing' that is pleasing in itself: flower colour becomes a bonus to be enjoyed in season, but not missed when absent. The interplay of contrasting leaf shapes, colours and textures and the overall shapes of plant masses can be infinitely varied and arranged to balance the harder lines of a man-made backdrop. The combination of shapes and textures here makes a particularly harmonious arrangement. Exciting schemes including coloured foliage add another dimension. 'Monochrome' themes of yellow-gold, purple and red, or silver and blue leaves can enhance the tones of hard materials nearby, and are enlivened by flower colour in season.

interest the viewer. Dramatic effects can be achieved by contrasting and harmonizing the vertically and horizontally 'shadowed' forms with all-over and neutral textures. Making a satisfying total picture is important when trees and shrubs are used for their textures alone, and when shrubs and plants have relatively short flowering periods so that their appearance during other seasons must be considered. (For more on planning flower colour schemes, see pages 162–3.)

Some plants have or can be given a clearly defined outline and you can use them architecturally to emphasize garden structure. Regular clipped evergreens, mop-headed trees, standard roses and so on are trained into distinctive shapes, and plants such as yuccas have an intrinsically architectural form. Leaf size and habit of growth can make plants ideal as the centre of a garden composition, or more fitted to supporting roles. Phormiums, irises and so on have vertical shadow-lines, for example. Many plants, however, are soft or rounded in appearance, and can act as a foil to the harder, regular lines and textures of man-made surfaces.

Just as with vibrant, eye-catching flower or foliage colour, strong positive plant shapes – such as fastigiate or conical

evergreens, with pronounced vertical shadow lines – need to be incorporated carefully into a garden, as part of a well-planned composition. On their own or associated with low flat plants they can make such abrupt statements that they appear like awkward exclamation marks. Their occasional value as focal points is undeniable, but the presence of several of them in a small garden can visually diminish the size of the plot in a dramatic way. The optical compulsion to use them as reference points and to keep measuring their relative positions induces a restless, unquiet mood.

A prime role of verticals is to act as screening, internally to separate different garden areas and, at the boundaries, to enclose the garden. The screening function is not necessarily most effectively done by erecting a dense, solid barrier. Using plants that are interesting in themselves is a better tactic. Thus a composition of the freer rounded forms of deciduous trees can make an attractive screen although it does not block out the view completely, whereas the distinctive shapes of a row of conical trees often direct attention to the very objects they are meant to screen – the eye is drawn to decipher what is beyond the grid pattern they create.

FOCAL POINTS

Focal points are extremely valuable for structure and interest in the garden. A focal point draws and arrests the attention. On a small scale it may be one particularly striking plant among an arrangement of others in a container; at the other extreme it might be some landmark at the end of an imposing vista. As a rule only one focal point should be in view at one time, since to see two or more sets up a conflict of interests and causes confusion and disharmony. But you can position a series of focal points so that having been drawn to examine one, the visitor then sees the next and is induced to move in that direction. Thus you can guide the visitor quite deliberately around a garden, possibly along a predetermined route. The quality of movement these tactics contribute is an essential in designing an interesting garden.

The effectiveness of a focal point depends as much on the way the item is sited and presented as on what it is. An object on a plinth or in a frame always draws the eye. One requirement is a neutral foil or backdrop which does not compete for attention – a smooth mass of evergreen foliage or a simple wall or fence, are ideal, as is a quiet expanse of open lawn around something like a specimen tree. The arrangement of the elements in the vicinity should provide the proper context – as when a focal point terminates the view at the end of a path or lawn. An object gains interest and importance when framed by some kind of archway, as does a statue in a niche.

Exactly what constitutes the focal point depends on the style of the garden as well as on individual taste. Ornaments and statues are favourites, and come in almost as many materials as forms. The range spans all manner of statues in the accepted sense, pieces of sculpture, vases, pots, planters, sundials, bird tables and so on in concrete, fibreglass, glass, marble, stone, wood, bronze, terracotta and ceramics. They are very much a personal choice, but must be appropriate to the garden. The statue of a Greek maiden in a romantic pose will appear incongruous in a modern, clean-lined setting as will a modern cylindrical concrete planter in a traditional or cottage garden. The impact made by an ornament or piece of sculpture should be neither overstated nor understated – though it is wise to err on the latter side.

Buildings and structures including summerhouses, gazebos, arbours and even glasshouses are potential focal points. A seat can be an ideal focus, with the additional attraction of offering rest to the visitor. However, a focal point need not be man-made. Plants in containers or as single specimens are suitable, provided that they stand out from their surroundings. Particularly useful are trees with a fastigiate or weeping habit, or which display distinctive characteristics, such as coloured bark, striking flowers or unusual leaves.

Some of the most successful focal points can lie outside the garden altogether – a beautiful view, a distant church tower or a lake all make legitimate eye-catchers. But be careful that the draw is not so strong that the elements within the garden itself fade to insignificance. When a view is the focal point, it sometimes needs to be framed by trees or shrubs so that a 'picture' is created.

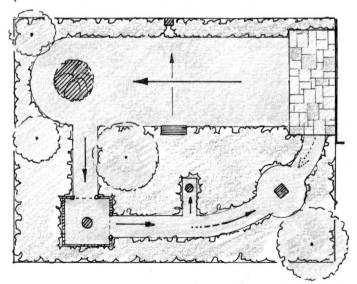

A succession of focal points draws you around this garden. Only the weeping tree is visible from the terrace; en route to it, and tucked away among shrubs, a seat faces an ornament across the lawn. On arrival at the tree, another focal point framed by trellised arches comes into view. From here a curving path leads back to the terrace via another object, and past a 'surprise'.

The field of vision surrounding a focal point needs to be kept simple so that nothing conflicts with the impact of the chosen object, allowing it to command full attention.

A church spire (top left), 'borrowed' for the focal point in a garden view, is framed by planting on either side, while the foreground is kept simple.

With the lines of a path converging on it, a doorway (centre left) is a focal point in itself. When the gate is tantalizingly left open, it offers an irresistible invitation to explore.

A seat (bottom left) draws the eye and urges the visitor to rest, with the promise of a fresh perspective and a view back over the route you have just taken.

A clipped hedge in the background and a straight path (top) display a sculptural piece in formal symmetry.

Buildings such as a summerhouse or gazebo (above) make satisfying focal points, their visual weight working well in informal layouts.

as screening 40, 78, 81, 83, 124
'sighting off' 134–5
site: detailed analysis of 8
    working within limits 20
site plan, making 11, 12, 32, 135–6
slate 123
    walls 140, 141
sloping gardens 14, 32, 51, 58–61, 70–3
    plotting levels 137
soil analysis 137
specialist garden 97
sports garden 124, 126–9
statues 51, 56, 147
    as focal points 18, 25, 27, 40
stepping stones 60, 62
    in gravel 82
    wooden 144
steps 85, 110, 127
    brick 31
    concealed lighting in 148
    concrete 95
    curved 60, 61, 71, 73
    in lawns 97
    linking levels 59
    natural stone 51, 60, 61, 71, 72
    in paths 74
    planning 12, 137, 146
    softening edges of 51
    on sloping site 51, 61, 71, 73
    timber 73, 146
    visually creating width 73
streams 78
styles: rule for small garden 40, 51
    using competing 20
summerhouse 10, 17, 31, 59, 73, 76, 86,
    99, 100, 119, 124, 132
    as changing room 127, 129
    as focal point 25, 26
sunbathing area 8, 10
sundials 49, 62, 69, 147
sunshine, effect on design 11
'surprises' 74, 76
surveying 134
swimming pools 90, 126–9
    siting 127
        checking orientation 137
    screening 128
symmetrical garden 30, 44, 49, 64, 106,
    129

Tennis court: siting 127, 129
terraces 28, 32, 56, 57, 61, 118
    doors opening on to 12
    echoing shape of 129
    enclosed 8
    help in building 152
    lighting on 74
    placing 51, 58, 60, 61, 71, 73, 74, 76, 80,
        82, 84, 97, 98, 100, 107, 114, 116,
        118, 121, 124, 127
    on plan 138

right proportions for 34
surrounding house 131, 132
viewpoint and 14
texture: and visual impact 24
    see also paving
themes: combining 27, 124
    overall 51
    Japanese 30
trees: adding height with 49, 62
    balancing design with 57, 67, 94, 123
    calculating scale of 34
    effect of oversized 34
    choosing: for dry shade 156
        for dry sun 154
        for exposed sites 158
        for moist shade 157
        for moist sun 155
        for seaside areas 157
        for total shade 155
        for water/bog garden 159
    clipped 28, 76, 77
    effect on balance 32
    espalier 78
    as focal points 25, 55, 68, 82, 127
        weeping 25, 47, 55, 57, 66, 97, 118,
            127
    matching 68, 69, 73, 84, 97, 100, 115,
        124, 128, 129, 131, 132
        for balance 110
        for depth 106
        rules for 32
    placing 7, 17, 24, 76, 81, 90, 98, 102,
        107, 111, 116, 127, 129, 132, 150
    pruning 21, 34
    roses to grow in 160
    as screens 11, 47, 51, 76, 78, 83, 92,
        102, 107, 119, 123, 124, 127, 129
        of boundaries 40, 49
    specimen 25, 73, 90, 112, 116, 124,
        128, 131
    visualizing when planning 14
    winter flowering 57, 76
trellis 20, 40, 78, 123, 143
'triangulation' 134, 136
trompe l'oeil 40, 49, 104

Underplanting 161

Vegetable garden 36, 53, 62, 64, 67, 83,
    112, 114–15, 116, 131, 132, 135, 139
    positioning 137, 138
vegetables, in ornamental garden 10
vertical elements 18, 32, 34, 92
    prime role of 21, 22, 24, 92
    see also fences; screens; trees
viewpoints: creating different 36
    importance when planning 14–15
visual impact 22–4
    assessing 20

Walkways 18, 131
walls 25, 40, 51, 53, 56, 70, 94, 111, 140–1
    adding extra height to 40
    breaking up expanses of 20, 40, 55, 59,
        84, 85
    concealed lighting in 148
    for defining spaces 18, 53
    help with building 152
    low, as seats 94
    materials 12, 22, 140–1, 142
    planning 140–2
        noting level changes 134, 137
    visual tricks with 42, 84, 102
    see also retaining walls
water features 30, 64, 68, 70, 71, 78,
    84–7, 102, 106, 116
    measuring 136
    planning for 10

see also canals; ponds/pools;
    fountains; streams
weather conditions: checking prevailing
    12
    effect on design 11
    see also wind
weeding 8, 10
weekend garden 100, 110
wheelchairs, design to accommodate
    83
wild/wildlife garden 10, 64, 88–91, 112,
    118–19
wind: checking prevailing 137
    providing shelter against 11
wind breaks 89, 123, 127
woodland garden 78, 121, 127
workshop, screening 131

USEFUL ADDRESSES

Blooms of Bressingham Ltd,
Bressingham Gardens,
Bressingham,
Diss,
Norfolk. IP22 2AB

The British Association of
Landscape Industries,
(Landscape Contractors Trade
Association),
Landscape House,
9 Henry Street,
Keighley,
West Yorkshire. BD21 3DR

The Building Centre,
26 Store Street,
London. WC1 E7BT
(advice on all building
materials; found also in all
major cities)

Centre on Environment for the
Handicapped,
35 Great Smith Street,
London. SW1P 3BJ

The College of Garden Design,
Hethersett,
Cothelstone,
Taunton,
Somerset. TA4 3DP

Aquatic Nurseries,
Gay Street,
Nr. Pulborough,
West Suffolk. RH20 2HH

The Institute of Horticulture,
80 Vincent Square,
London. SW1P 2PE

Notcutts Nurseries Ltd,
Woodbridge,
Suffolk. IP12 4AF

The Royal Horticultural
Society,
80 Vincent Square,
London. SW1P 2PE

The Society of Landscape and
Garden Designers,
23 Reigate Road,
Ewell, Surrey. KT17 1PS

ACKNOWLEDGMENTS

Author's Acknowledgments

I would like to thank Frances Lincoln for inviting me to write and illustrate *The Garden Planner*. Grateful thanks also to her dedicated team of skilful and helpful editors and designers, in particular Caroline Hillier, Louise Tucker, Sarah Mitchell and Erica Hunningher. My wife Ann typed the manuscript and notes and gave great support and encouragement without which this book would not have been written. Lastly my sincere thanks to Notcutts Nurseries of Woodbridge, Suffolk; Bressingham Gardens of Diss, Norfolk and Anthony Archer-Wills of Aquatic Nurseries, Sussex for their generous advice on plants.

Publishers Acknowledgments

The Publishers would like to thank the following people for their help in producing this book: Penny David for editorial contributions; Tony Lord for horticultural contributions; and Emma Callery, Anne Fisher, Katy Foskew, Nicola Medlikova, Susan Nice, Stephen Riddle and Karen Watson for editorial and design assistance.

Editor	Sarah Mitchell
Art Editor	Louise Tucker
Editorial Director	Erica Hunningher
Art Director	Caroline Hillier
Picture Editor	Anne Fraser

Photographic Acknowledgments

Heather Angel 11 and 91 (Chris Baines)
Boys Syndication/Michael Boys 93, 111, Jacqui Hurst 54, 82
Geoff Dann FLL © 51, 61
Karl-Dietrich Buhler 33
Garden Picture Library/Henk Dijkman 117, Anthony Paul 156, Gary Rogers 101, Wolfram Stehling 79, Ron Sutherland 8, 32, 45, 86, 106, 107, 120, 151, Kate Zari 23
Jerry Harpur 13, 35, 36–7 (Lucy Gent), 41, 60, 110, 121, 144
Marijke Heuff 17 (Ineke Greve), 28–9 and front cover (Mr & Mrs van Rappard-Elias)
Roger Hillier 113 (Jean Sugden)
Jacqui Hurst FLL © 103 (Mrs Ruth Barclay), 125
Andrew Lawson 3 (Mrs Whittington), 16 left, middle, right, 30, 65 (Lucy Gent), 72 left and right (Mrs Whittington)
Marianne Majerus FLL © 31
S & O Mathews Photography 9, 15
Tania Midgley FLL © 68 top
Phillipe Perdereau 19
Elizabeth Whiting & Associates/Karl-Dietrich Buhler 68 bottom, Michael Dunne 149, Andreas von Einsiedel 21, Jerry Harpur 27 (Gail Jenkins), 38 (Helen Preston), 77, 96, 100, 147, Rodney Hyett 128, Jerry Tubby 10
Steve Wooster FLL © 150 (Beth Chatto)

Garden Designers

Michael Balston 32, Richard Bodeker 13, 35, 60, 110, 121, Valtin von Delius 33, Arno King 146, Gail Jenkins 27, Anthony Paul 86, Duane Paul Design Team 45, 142, Christopher Masson 41, Pietor Plomin 120, Michael Runge 144, Mark Rumary 147, Mien Ruys 106, Alan Sargent 72 left, Henk Weijers 117, Robin Williams 68 (top)